Teacher's Guide

Green Level

A Harcourt Achieve Imprint

www.Rigby.com
1-800-531-5015

Rigby PM Science Readers
Teacher's Guide, Green Level

Harcourt Achieve Inc.
10801 N. Mopac Exp.
Building 3
Austin, Texas 78759
www.harcourtachieve.com

1 2 3 4 5 6 7 8 9 862 10 09 08 07 06

Printed in the United States

ISBN 1-4189-4230-8

Contents

Meticulously Leveled Books promote reading success!

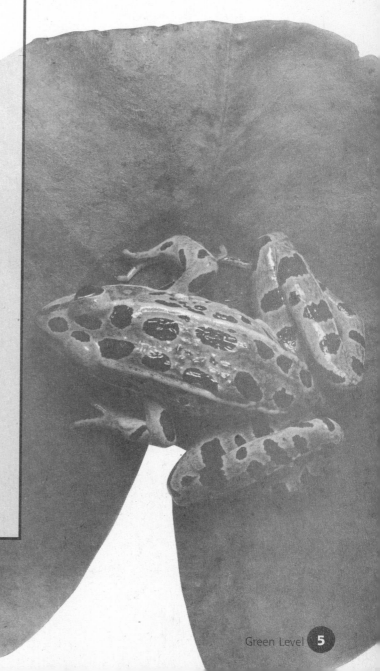

- **Captivating science** with topics that are egocentric to the science world of young readers

- **Low ratio** of 1:20 new word inclusion provides a systematic introduction of high-frequency words for young readers

- **Steady growth** of sentence structures scaffolds text complexity for incremental success

- **Meaningful stories** with a clear climax and resolution hook children with real storylines

- **Repetition and review** of high-frequency words assists readers with building and using a storehouse of known words

A New Addition to the PM Family!

Captivating Science through Leveled Reading!

Red Level
Exploring My World

Yellow Level
Animals in My World

> "Literature can help students connect personally to scientific ideas by setting science in familiar and meaningful contexts." (Griffiths and Clyne, 1991)

Blue Level
Exploring My Senses

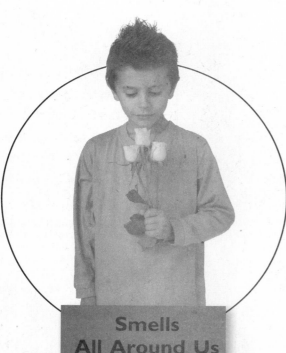

Green Level
Exploring My Planet

A Consistent Instructional Path...

Provides a single clear foundation for the entire *PM* Family:

1 **Small Group Strategy Instruction** allows for personalized teaching, step-by-step.

2 **Informal Assessment** provides teachers the opportunity to evaluate each child before moving on to the next text.

Use the *PM Ultra Benchmark Kit* to:

- **START** the year by placing children in texts at their instructional reading level;

- **CHECK** at intervals during the year how children are progressing through the levels;

- **MONITOR** children's progress throughout the year to inform instruction.

3

Independent Practice

lets children build on their success through a variety of activities.

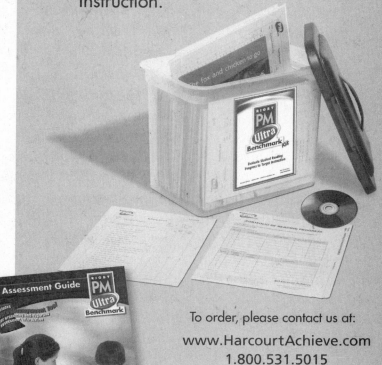

To order, please contact us at:
www.HarcourtAchieve.com
1.800.531.5015

Leveled Texts Plus Guided Lessons

Teacher's Guide
Green Level

Life in Hot Places

Julie Haydon

Stars in the Sky

Julie Haydon

Equals Components for Success!

4 Color Levels

PM Science Readers books are grouped into 4 color levels — Red, Yellow, Blue, and Green. Each group contains ten titles that provide various opportunities for reading success.

PM Reading Levels

Across the *PM Science Readers* series, reading skills are introduced incrementally from the emergent to the early reader levels. This meticulous leveling promotes reading success by leading readers through accomplishments step-by-step.

PM Levels

1
2
3
4
5
6
7
8
9
12
13 14
15
18
19
20
21
22
23
24

Rigby®

A Harcourt Achieve Imprint

RIGBY PM SCIENCE READERS

Step-by-step Lessons...

Ensure thorough instruction of focused strategies, skills, and vocabulary words.

> An introductory box provides a quick overview of the book as well as skills taught in the lesson.

> Challenging concepts or skills are supported for English Language Learners through extended activities.

We Need the Sun

Written by Heather Hammonds

Overview The sun is important to life on Earth. It gives us heat and light. Some times of the year are warmer than others.

Reading Vocabulary Words daytime p. 4, autumn p. 8, nighttime p. 14

Phonics Skill Compound words

Fluency Point Reading smoothly

Comprehension Strategy Connecting text-to-self

Reading Strategy Checking for a pattern

Reading Word Count: 202

High-Frequency Words

end	live
every	warm
grow	when

1 Before Reading

Build Background
- Introduce the book by reading the title, talking about the cover photograph, and sharing the overview.
- Explain to children that as they read the text, they should think of how the story connects to their life. Say *This book is about the sun.* Ask *How does the sun affect you? Do you prefer sunny days or cloudy days? Do you like nighttime or daytime better? Making a connection to the book will help you understand what you are reading.*
- Have children share what they know about the sun. Ask them to describe the sun.

Focus on Reading Vocabulary
- Write *autumn* on chart paper. Read the word aloud. Have children use the word in a sentence. Next, write *daytime* and *nighttime.* Read the words aloud. Ask *How are these words similar? Yes, they both have the word time in them.*
- Model filling in a Word Sorter. Write *daytime* in the top box. Have children name two words that are different for the next level, such as *animals* and *people.* The lower three boxes will have examples of daytime animals (cows, dogs, birds) and daytime people (children, mail carrier, bus driver).

Focus on Phonics Compound words
- Write *sun/rise* on chart paper. Explain that some words are made from two words. Readers can divide compound words into smaller, familiar words to help read these long words. Ask children to name another compound word with the word *sun* (*sunset*).
- Have children suggest three other compound words with *sun.* Write each suggested word on the chart. (*sunshine, sunburn, suntan, sunflower*) Draw a line to show the division of the words.

Science Standard:
- Knows that the sun provides heat and light to Earth
- Light, heat, electricity, and magnetism

Focus on Fluency
- Read page 2 aloud. First, read with unnatural interruptions. Ask *Was I reading smoothly?* Say *Reading smoothly helps you understand better.* Read page 2 in a natural manner. Ask *How was that better?*
- Have children select a page from the book. Have them read to a partner to see if they are reading smoothly. Have children practice until their reading is smooth.

Focus on Comprehension
- Explain that every reader can connect what he or she reads to his or her own experiences. Have children look at pages 4–5. Ask *Do you like getting up in the morning? Do you like to get up at sunrise or later in the day?* Have children look at pages 6 and 9. Ask *Which of these activities do you prefer? Why? Do you like to be in the sunshine or indoors? Why?*

2 Reading the Text

Book Talk
Cover	Read aloud the title with children. Point out the author's name. Talk about how hot the sun looks and the colors of the sunset.
Pages 2–3	Say *I am noticing how big the sun is compared to **Earth**. What does the sun give us? Yes, it gives us light and warmth.*
Pages 4–5	Ask *What is the boy doing? Yes, he is waking up. It is daytime. What other animals get up at **sunrise**?*
Pages 6–7	Say *I see a beach with people. What time of year is it? Yes, it's summer. How does the sun feel in the summer? Yes, it's hot.*
Pages 8–9	Say *I am noticing other seasons. This pattern of giving information helps me with my reading. In which season does it snow?*
Pages 10–11	Say *This picture shows plants that are getting a lot of sun. What compound word do you see that describes the sun? Yes, sunshine. The sun is shining on the garden.*
Pages 12–13	Ask *What kind of place is this? Yes, a desert. There is not much growing there. Do you think it is hot there all the time?*
Pages 14–15	Say *The sun is setting. What time of day is it? Yes, it will be nighttime. What do you do at nighttime?*

ESL-ELL tip

Before reading the book, help children understand that many English words are compound words. A compound word is two or more words written as one word. Have children go through the book and find the following compound words: *sunshine, daytime, nighttime, sunset.* Help them divide the words.

Reading Strategy

Remind children of the skills and strategies when assistance is needed. Say *Sometimes you will see repeated words or phrases that form patterns. Check patterns as you read.*

Green Level

> Two Science standards are connected with each title — a combined-state and a National Science Education Standard.

> Identified by the open book icon, reading strategies are tailored to the emergent and early reader.

Individual differences in children are addressed by offering activities for two or more of the following learning styles: kinesthetic, auditory, visual, and tactile.

Individual Reading

Have each child read the whole book at his or her own pace while remaining in the group. Observe children as they read. Make note, mentally or in writing, how each child is or is not using the skills and strategies being focused on in this lesson:

1. Are children able to identify and read the reading vocabulary words without assistance?
2. Are children able to identify and read compound words?
3. Are children reading smoothly to improve comprehension?
4. Are children making text-to-self connections while reading?
5. Are children checking for patterns when reading?

3 Text Reading Review

Reading Vocabulary Review

- Have children draw a daytime scene and a nighttime scene on different sheets of paper. Have them label their drawings. Share the drawings with the class and have children say the corresponding words.
- Have children highlight, or add, the reading vocabulary words in their copies of *My PM Word Book*. Encourage children to use these words in their writing.

Phonics Review

Write *sometimes* on chart paper. Have children say the two smaller words and write them on chart paper: *some + times*. Add the following words: *sunrise, daytime, sunshine, nighttime, sunset*. Have children write the two words as you did on their own paper. Write the correct divisions on the chart paper.

Fluency Review

Have children reread several pages from the book with a partner. Remind children to read smoothly. Encourage children to practice reading the same pages until they are reading as though they were talking.

Comprehension Review

Have children reread the book in pairs. Have partners share if they prefer daytime, with the sun out, or nighttime. Remind children that making connections between themselves and the text helps with their reading.

Connection for Writing

Have each child create a visual chart for each season. Have him or her write a phrase, using the same pattern as in the book, that describes how much sun Earth is getting.

nect to Math

Math Readers
g a Clock Cake
7–18)
children, draw a clock
hat represents the
he sun rises and sets.
computer to find out
times for your area.

M Science Readers
eacher's Guide

4 Assessment and Practice

Reading Vocabulary Application

Provide children with a Word Sorter with the word *nighttime* in the top box. Work with children to name two activities they do at nighttime in the next level of boxes. Have children describe each activity on the appropriate side of the organizer.

Phonics Evaluation

Write *night, day, snow,* and *rain* on chart paper. With children, brainstorm a list of compound words that begin with these words. Ask volunteers to provide a sentence with a word from the list.

Fluency Assessment

Individually, have each child read the story to you. Check for smooth reading.

Comprehension Check

Individually, have each child share which season he or she prefers and why.

Independent Practice

- Have children practice the high-frequency words found within this title using the matching PM High-Frequency Word Cards.
- Provide children with a copy of the activity sheet. Give directions on how to complete the activity sheet. Have children complete the sheet independently.

Differentiated Instruction

- **Kinesthetic** learners can "feel" the story by stepping outside to feel the sun and providing the class with a weather report.
- **Auditory** learners can "hear" the story by listening to songs about sunny days or rainy days.
- **Visual** learners can "see" the story by drawing illustrations that show how the sun heats and lights Earth.

Answer Key

every day	In spring and summer
in the morning	all the time
on hot days	at the end of the day

The sun comes up __every day__
__In spring and summer__

there are lots of sunny days.
We stay out of the sun __on hot days__

In some places,
it is very hot and sunny __all the time__

The sun shines __in the morning__

The sun goes down __at the end of the day__

Nighttime
- eat dinner — salad, milk, meatloaf
- play games with my brother — fun (easy), relaxing

Answers will vary.

Math and Science concepts are linked between PM leveled reading programs with content area foci.

Accurate and possible answers are provided for both reproducible graphic organizers.

Additional Resources...

Build a POWERFUL Solution for Differentiating and Documenting Learning

PM Resources

includes hundreds of leveled books in the *PM Collection/Platinum, PM Plus, PM Math Readers,* and *PM Photo Stories* series.

My PM Word Book

is a consumable paperback with alphabetically sorted vocabulary words that children can refer to while writing.

Reading Strategies Tool Kit

is a unique, supplemental instructional tool kit with convenient, easy-to-use Reading Strategies Cards that provide research-based, visually supported differentiated instruction in the five key pillars of reading.

PM Ultra Benchmark K

is an effective assessment tool Grades K–5 that can be used place a child in the appropri level of PM Resources and Rigby Flying Colors series. Da gathered during an assessme can be entered into the softwa for classroom, school, and district use.

Writing Tool Kit

is a supplemental instruction tool that offers explicit strategy instruction in three key areas of writing: writing process, writing traits, and writing forms.

PM High-Frequency Word Cards

include everything you need to help children learn critical sight words at school and home — building a foundation for reading success!

To order, please contact us at:
www.HarcourtAchieve.com
1.800.531.5015

The following standards can be found throughout the *PM Science Readers* program:

Science Standard	RED	YELLOW	BLUE	GREEN
Systems, order, and organization	🔍		🔍	
Form and function			🔍	
Properties of objects and materials	🔍		🔍🔍	
Light, heat, electricity, and magnetism				🔍
Characteristics of organisms	🔍	🔍🔍🔍🔍🔍🔍	🔍	
Life cycles of organisms	🔍			
Organisms and environments	🔍🔍	🔍🔍🔍		🔍🔍
Properties of earth materials	🔍🔍			🔍🔍
Objects in the sky				🔍🔍
Changes in earth and sky	🔍🔍			
Abilities of technological design			🔍🔍	
Personal health			🔍	
Types of resources		🔍		
Changes in environments			🔍🔍	🔍🔍🔍

• Each magnifying glass represents a title within marked color level.

Lessons

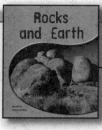

Rocks and Earth

Written by Heather Hammonds

Overview Rocks and their different sizes and locations are described. Children learn about river rocks, boulders and mountains, and hot rocks that lie under the earth. Collecting rocks is fun and educational.

Reading Vocabulary Words garden p. 3, mountains p. 4, wave p. 6

Phonics Skill Use knowledge of spelling patterns: CVC*e*

Fluency Point Adjusting pace

Comprehension Strategy Classifying and categorizing information

Reading Strategy Looking at pictures

Reading Word Count: 196

High-Frequency Words

ask	sometimes
these	everyone
keep	under

1 Before Reading

Build Background

- Introduce the book by reading the title, talking about the cover photograph, and sharing the overview.
- Remind children that looking at pictures can help them read the text. Say *Pictures have information about the book's subject. Sometimes the pictures can help you figure out some unknown words. Pictures can also help you visualize what the author is writing about.*
- Ask children if anyone has a rock collection. Have them discuss how they collect rocks. Have children share if they have ever been hiking and seen some unusual rock formations.

Focus on Reading Vocabulary

- Write each vocabulary word on sheets of paper and read them aloud. Have children draw simple pictures of the vocabulary words. Then ask them to make up sentences about rocks using the vocabulary words.
- Model filling in a Sentence Maker. Write *garden* in the oval. Ask *What do gardens look like? What do they have in them? What else grows in gardens?* Have children write three sentences with *garden*.

Focus on Phonics Spelling pattern: CVC*e*

- Write *made* and *wave* on chart paper. Read the words aloud. Point out that both words have a similar spelling pattern: consonant, vowel, consonant, and a silent *e*. Explain that the silent *e* can change the sound of the middle vowel. *(mad/made, hop/hope)*
- Have children name additional words that follow the CVC*e* spelling pattern. Write each suggested word, and use each word in a sentence as you are writing them. *(cave, give, have, live, same, some, bike)*

Science Standard:

- **Knows the properties of substances can change when they are cooled or heated**
- **Properties of earth materials**

Focus on Fluency

- Read aloud pages 2–3, modeling how you adjust your pace for periods and repeated words. Ask *Did you notice how I did not rush through the sentences? I adjusted my pace to pause for periods. I read some sentences more slowly and others more quickly. The changes make my reading more interesting.*
- Partner children and have them read pages 2–3, making sure they are adjusting their pace as they read.

Focus on Comprehension

- Explain that readers think about what they are reading and group the information by similar features. Say *As you read, try to group information together by finding things that are the same. This book is about rocks.* Say *As you read, notice how rocks can be grouped together.*

2   Reading the Text

Book Talk

Cover   Read aloud the title with children. Point out the author's name. Talk about the color, size, texture, and weight of these big rocks.

Pages 2–3   Say *This boy has a **rock collection.** Does anyone collect rocks? What colors are some of his rocks? Yes, I see red, blue, and green, too!*

Pages 4–5   Say *I see different sizes of rocks and mountains. Where are the small rocks? Yes, in the river. Have you ever seen such big rocks?*

Pages 6–7   Say *These rocks have interesting shapes. What do they look like? Yes, one looks like a wave. One looks like a cake!*

Pages 8–9   Say *I see rocks in a river. Did you know rocks were under the sea, too? How many of you have seen rocks in a cave?*

Pages 10–11   Say *This picture shows hot rock inside the earth. It is so hot it flows!* Ask *What happens when hot rock reaches cool air? Yes, it gets hard.*

Pages 12–13   Say *These children are looking at rocks in a **museum.** Have you ever seen such a large collection of rocks? Look at all the shapes and colors.*

Pages 14–15   Ask *What do you need to start your own rock collection? Yes, you need a box, some rocks, and a magnifying glass. How does the picture help you know what you need to get started?*

ESL-ELL tip

Before reading the book, help children understand that the word *wave* can be used in two ways. Tell children that in the book, *wave* is used to describe a shape of a rock, which looks like a wave that the ocean makes (show a picture). A person can also *wave* (show gesture) to a friend.

Reading Strategy

Remind children of the skills and strategies when assistance is needed. Say *Looking at the pictures can help you figure out what a word might be.*

Individual Reading

Have each child read the whole book at his or her own pace while remaining in the group. Observe children as they read. Make note, mentally or in writing, how each child is or is not using the skills and strategies being focused on in this lesson:

1. Are children able to identify and read the reading vocabulary words without assistance?
2. Are children able to use knowledge of spelling pattern CVC*e* to read?
3. Are children adjusting their pace as they read?
4. Are children classifying and categorizing information while reading?
5. Are children looking at pictures as aids when reading?

3   Text Reading Review

Reading Vocabulary Review

- Write the words *mountain* and *garden* on chart paper. Have children draw a mountain with a garden nearby. Have them label their drawing.
- Have children highlight, or add, the reading vocabulary words in their copies of *My PM Word Book*. Encourage children to use these words in their writing.

Phonics Review

Write *hug, mad,* and *pin* on chart paper. Have children say the words aloud. Then add *e* to each word: *huge, made, pine*. Add to the chart paper. Have children say the new words aloud. Next, have children say the words in pairs: *hug, huge,* and so on. Discuss how the silent *e* changes the sound of the middle vowel. Remind children to notice the silent *e* when reading.

Fluency Review

Have children take turns rereading sections of the book with a partner. Some sentences should be read more slowly. Remind children to adjust their pace.

Comprehension Review

Show children how to divide a sheet of paper into thirds. Have them work with a partner and find at least three ways to group rocks together. Remind children to look for common features. (on land, underwater, in the earth, size, color)

Connection for Writing

Have each child write a list of what he or she needs to start a rock collection. At the end of the list, have him or her write three sentences explaining the steps he or she will follow to get started.

Connect to Math

PM Math Readers
Fourteen Marbles
(Set 16–17)
With children, look at rocks from the book. Decide how many ways they can group rocks together. Make a list of the different ways in which rocks can be categorized.

4 Assessment and Practice

Reading Vocabulary Application

Provide children with a copy of the Sentence Maker with *mountains* written in the oval. Work with children to write different sentences with the word *mountains* and fill in the ovals.

Phonics Evaluation

Have children write *wave, wake, made, some, like,* and *care* on separate index cards. Ask children to take turns showing their cards to their partner and asking their partner to read aloud the word on each card.

Fluency Assessment

Individually, have each child read a section of the book to you. Listen to see that children are adjusting their pace as they read.

Comprehension Check

Have children reread the book and look at the pictures. Have them tell you ways in which rocks can be grouped together.

Independent Practice

- Have children practice the high-frequency words found within this title using the matching PM High-Frequency Word Cards.
- Provide children with a copy of the activity sheet. First children complete sentences about rocks. Then they find the right verb to start each sentence. To practice sequence skills, have children insert a number in the box to the left of each sentence.

Differentiated Instruction

- **Kinesthetic** learners can "feel" the story by collecting a few rocks and showing the class how the size and texture varies.
- **Auditory** learners can "hear" the story by listening to someone else reading the book to them.
- **Visual** learners can "see" the story by drawing an illustration of hot rock (lava) flowing from a volcano.

Answer Key

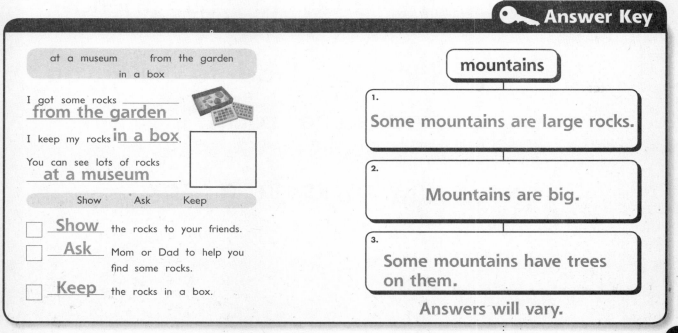

at a museum   from the garden
in a box

I got some rocks _____
from the garden .

I keep my rocks **in a box** .

You can see lots of rocks
at a museum .

Show   Ask   Keep

☐ **Show** the rocks to your friends.

☐ **Ask** Mom or Dad to help you find some rocks.

☐ **Keep** the rocks in a box.

mountains

1. Some mountains are large rocks.

2. Mountains are big.

3. Some mountains have trees on them.

Answers will vary.

Name_____

at a museum   from the garden

in a box

I got some rocks _____

_____ .

I keep my rocks _____ .

You can see lots of rocks

_____ .

Show   Ask   Keep

☐ _____ the rocks to your friends.

☐ _____ Mom or Dad to help you
find some rocks.

☐ _____ the rocks in a box.

Name_____

Sentence Maker

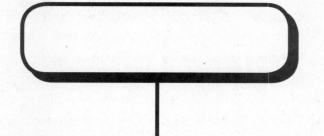

1.

2.

3.

My Book of the Seasons

Written by Julie Haydon

Overview A girl makes a book about the four seasons. What she eats, what she does, and what she wears change with each season. The weather changes, too.

Reading Vocabulary Words magazines p. 2, sandals p. 5, autumn p. 7, jacket p. 8

Phonics Skill Changing phonemes to make new words

Fluency Point Using softness or loudness to express emotion

Comprehension Strategy Connecting text-to-self

Reading Strategy Thinking about what comes next and if it makes sense

**Reading
Word Count: 271**

High-Frequency Words

about	cool
give	hot
short	warm

1   Before Reading

Build Background

- Introduce the book by reading the title, talking about the cover photograph, and sharing the overview.
- Remind children that they can use their reading voice to show emotions. Say *You can show the way someone in a story is feeling. Here's how! You use your loud voice like this* (sound happy, excited): "We had so much fun at the playground!" *You use your soft voice like this* (sound factual): "Each season lasts three months."
- Ask *Have you ever made a book about what you see in the world around you?* Have children discuss the seasons. Ask *What do you do in the summer that you cannot do in the winter?*

Focus on Reading Vocabulary

- Write each vocabulary word on chart paper. Read aloud each word. Ask *Which word is something you can read?* (magazine) *Which word is something you can wear?* (jacket, sandals) *Which word is part of a year?* (autumn)
- Model filling in a Word Map. Write *magazine* in the diamond. Ask *Where can you find magazines?* and fill in the "Give examples!" boxes. Have children describe a *magazine,* and fill in the "Describe it!" ovals.

Focus on Phonics Changing phonemes to make new words

- Write *book, hot, long, hat,* and *beach* on chart paper. Read the words aloud. Say *I can change the first letter of each word and make a new word.* Model by writing *hook* beneath *book.* Underline *b* and *h.* Emphasize the sound of each letter as you say both words aloud again.
- Have children suggest other letters that they can change in the remaining words to make new words. (*dot, song, mat, reach*)

Science Standard:

- Knows that the weather changes over the seasons and on a daily basis
- Changes in environments

Focus on Fluency

- Read aloud page 4, modeling how you change your voice to show emotion. Say *Changing my voice makes the reading more interesting.* Ask *When was my voice loud?* (Sometimes I eat ice cream.) *What was I feeling then?* (happy, excited)
- Partner children and have them alternate reading aloud page 4. Make sure they are using softness or loudness to express emotion.

Focus on Comprehension

- Explain that readers think about how what they are reading relates to their own experiences. Say *As you read, think about how things change for you in each season.*

2   Reading the Text

Book Talk

Cover   Read aloud the title with children. Point out the girl holding her own book. Talk about the pictures on her book cover and the seasons they represent. (cloud, winter; sun, summer; tree, fall; flower/bee, spring)

Pages 2–3   Say *First the girl tells us how she made her book about the seasons. I see different-colored pencils and a glue stick.* Ask *What do you see? Yes, there is a pile of* **magazines** *with colorful pictures.*

Pages 4–5   Say *This part of her book is about summer. Can you tell by looking at the pictures? Yes, there is a sunny beach,* **sandals**, *and a hat.*

Pages 6–7   Say *Here we go from summer into autumn. Which picture tells you it's autumn? Yes, the leaves. Look at their colors. The leaves are no longer green when they fall off the tree.*

Pages 8–9   Say *I wear a* **jacket** *when it gets cool outside. Look at the girl's feet. Are those sandals? No, she's wearing shoes now.* Ask *What do you see in the pictures of the trees? Yes, there are leaves all over the ground. Have you ever walked through a pile of leaves? It's fun!*

Pages 10–11   Say *Brrr! That photograph sure looks cold. But isn't the snow pretty?* Ask *What is the girl wearing on her feet? Yes, she's wearing boots. Good thing she has mittens, a warm hat, and a scarf to put on, too!*

Pages 12–13   Say *It looks like they're making a doll house.* Ask *What are some other things you could make to play with in winter?*

Pages 14–15   Ask *What do flowers need to grow? Yes, sunshine and water. They need warm days, too. That's why flowers bloom in the spring.*

Individual Reading

Have each child read the whole book at his or her own pace while remaining in the group. Observe children as they read. Make note, mentally or in writing, how each child is or is not using the skills and strategies being focused on in this lesson:

1. Are children able to identify and read the reading vocabulary words without assistance?
2. Are children able to change phonemes to make new words?
3. Are children using softness or loudness to express emotion?
4. Are children making text-to-self connections as they read?
5. Are children thinking about what comes next and if it makes sense?

3 Text Reading Review

Reading Vocabulary Review

- Write the words *autumn* and *jacket* on chart paper. Have children draw themselves wearing a jacket in autumn. Have them label their drawings.
- Have children highlight, or add, the reading vocabulary words in their copies of *My PM Word Book*. Encourage children to use these words in their writing.

Phonics Review

Write these high-frequency words on chart paper: *cool, hot, short,* and *warm.* Beneath each word write *pool, pot, sport,* and *warp.* Ask *What letters did I change in each word to make a new word? What is the new sound in each new word? That's right, the pah sound.* Invite volunteers to underline the phoneme changed in the original word. (*cool, hot, short, warm*)

Fluency Review

Have children take turns rereading sections of the book with a partner. Some sentences should be read more loudly to express emotion.

Comprehension Review

Show children how to divide a sheet of paper into fourths. Have them label each section *spring, summer, autumn,* and *winter.* In each section, have children list at least three things that change for them in that season.

Connection for Writing

Have each child write a list of what he or she needs to make a book of the seasons. At the end of the list, have him or her write three to four sentences explaining the steps he or she will follow to make the book. Remind each child to use the four-fold seasons sheet from the Comprehension Review activity.

Connect to Math

PM Math Readers

Billy's Sticker Book
(Set D/15–16)
Help children categorize seasons with seasonal items. Using index cards instead of stickers, children can draw small pictures to represent each season. Have children draw three pictures for each season. By sharing their index cards, children can work together to copy the groupings on page 16.

4 Assessment and Practice

Reading Vocabulary Application

Provide children with a copy of the Word Map with *autumn* written in the diamond. Work with children to fill in the "Give examples!" boxes. Ask *When does autumn happen?* Have children describe autumn and fill in the "Describe it!" ovals. Ask *How do you know when it's autumn?*

Phonics Evaluation

Ask *How can I turn a hat into a bat?* Let children tell you which letter change makes the new word. For each of the following word pairs, have children identify the different sound in each new word: *book/took, hot/lot, long/lung,* and *beach/peach.*

Fluency Assessment

Individually, have each child read a section of the book to you. Listen to see that each child modulates loudness and softness of voice to express emotion.

Comprehension Check

Have children reread the book and look at the pictures. Have them tell you how they experience a particular season.

Independent Practice

- Have children practice the high-frequency words found within this title using the matching PM High-Frequency Word Cards.
- Provide children with a copy of the activity sheet. Give directions on how to complete the activity sheet. Have children complete the sheet independently.

Differentiated Instruction

- **Kinesthetic** learners can "feel" the story by collecting items that remind them of each season.
- **Auditory** learners can "hear" the story by imagining the different sounds they hear in each season.
- **Visual** learners can "see" the story by drawing pictures of how they experience each season.

Answer Key

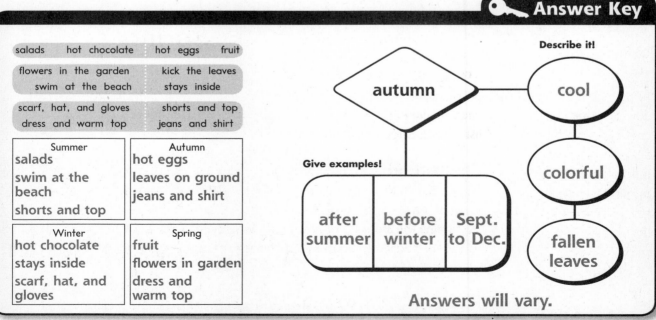

| salads | hot chocolate | hot eggs | fruit |

| flowers in the garden swim at the beach | kick the leaves stays inside |

| scarf, hat, and gloves dress and warm top | shorts and top jeans and shirt |

Summer
salads
swim at the beach
shorts and top

Autumn
hot eggs
leaves on ground
jeans and shirt

Winter
hot chocolate
stays inside
scarf, hat, and gloves

Spring
fruit
flowers in garden
dress and warm top

Describe it!

autumn

Give examples!

after summer | before winter | Sept. to Dec.

cool

colorful

fallen leaves

Answers will vary.

Name_____

salads   hot chocolate   ┊   hot eggs   fruit

flowers in the garden   ┊   kick the leaves
swim at the beach   ┊   stays inside

scarf, hat, and gloves   ┊   shorts and top
dress and warm top   ┊   jeans and shirt

Summer	Autumn

Winter	Spring

Name _____

Word Map

Describe it!

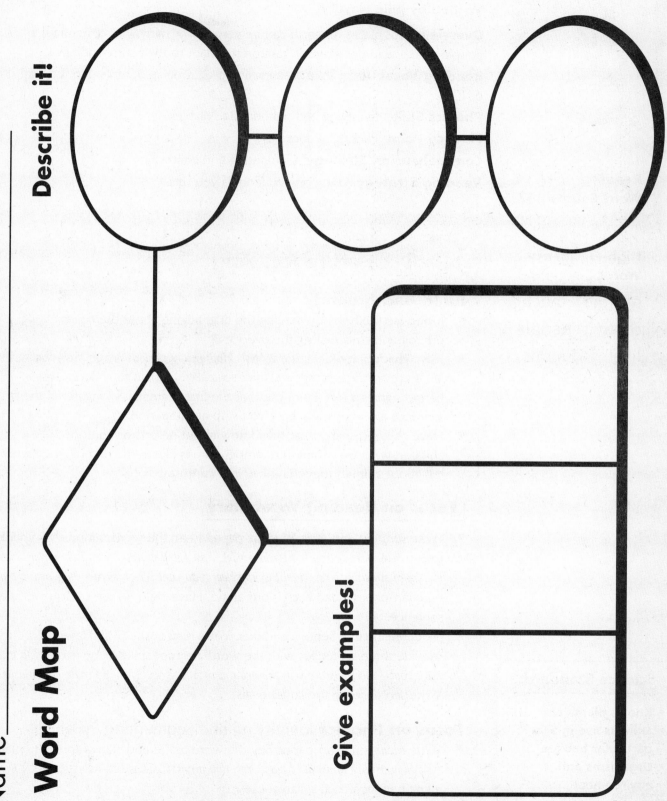

Give examples!

Life in Hot Places

Written by Julie Haydon

Overview Hot places on earth can be very dry or rainy. Plants, animals, and people who live in deserts or in rainforests adapt to their surroundings.

Reading Vocabulary Words sunshine p. 2, roots p. 5, tents p. 6, tropical p. 10

Phonics Skill Identifying and segmenting syllables

Fluency Point Pausing at commas

Comprehension Strategy Comparing and contrasting

Reading Strategy Using punctuation as you read

Reading Word Count: 247

High-Frequency Words

ground	much
grow	people
live	under

Science Standard:

- **Knows plants and animals live in a particular habitat**
- **Organisms and environment**

1 Before Reading

Build Background

- Introduce the book by reading the title, talking about the cover photograph, and sharing the overview.
- Have children look at page 2. Ask *How many periods are on this page? Yes, there are three periods and three sentences.* Explain to children that a period signals a rest. Point out that the first sentence is long. Read the first sentence aloud to show how you stop at the period.
- Have children share what they know about deserts or rainforests. Ask children what they think the temperature is like in the desert. Ask them to tell about animals they think live in a rainforest.

Focus on Reading Vocabulary

- Write *sunshine* and *tents* on chart paper. Read the words aloud. Ask children to provide a sentence for each word. Ask *How would a tent help when there is a lot of sunshine? Yes, a tent would keep you cool.* Then write *roots* and *tropical* on chart paper. Read each word aloud. Have children use each word in a sentence.
- Model filling in a Sentence Maker. Write *roots* in the oval. Have children provide three sentences with the word. Prompt children by asking *Do trees have roots? Do roots grow in the ground or in the air? How do roots help plants?* Write sentences in the larger ovals.

Focus on Phonics Identifying and Segmenting Syllables

- Write *cactus* on chart paper. Say the word aloud and clap with each syllable. Ask *How many times did I clap? Yes, two times.* Cactus *has two syllables.* Draw a line between each syllable: cac/tus.
- Write *tropical, rainforest,* and *village* on chart paper. Say each word aloud. Have children repeat each word and clap with each syllable. Show children where the syllables break. (trop/i/cal, rain/for/est, vil/lage)

Focus on Fluency

- Have children look at page 8. Ask *What punctuation do you see other than periods? Yes, there are commas.* Say *Commas are a signal to make a slight pause in reading.* Model reading the sentences aloud.
- Write *In the daytime* on chart paper. Have children suggest what they do in the daytime. Complete the sentence. Ask *Where does the comma go? Yes, after* daytime.

Focus on Comprehension

- Explain that readers look to find similar and different features about things when they read. Have children look at pages 2–3. Say *These pictures show two different places, but they are alike because they are both hot places.* With children, fill in a Venn diagram to contrast and compare the two places.

2 Reading the Text

Book Talk

Cover

Read aloud the title with children. Point out the author's name. Ask children what they do when it is hot outside.

Pages 2–3

Say *Both of these places are hot.* Ask *Which place gets more rain? Yes, the rainforest. Does the desert get much rain? No, it does not.*

Pages 4–5

Say *This is a desert.* Ask *What kind of plants grow in the desert? Yes, cactus. Do you think the sand and rocks are hot? Yes, they would be.*

Pages 6–7

Say *People who live in the desert cover their bodies to stay cool. They move to be near water. See the water. It looks refreshing. The trees make **shade**, which helps keep things cool, too.*

Pages 8–9

Say *Desert animals sleep during the day and hunt at night. Why do they sleep all day? Yes, it's too hot in the sun. Look at the camel. Where does it store water? Yes, in its hump.*

Pages 10–11

Say *Look at this tropical forest. Does it look like it would be hot? Tropical forests are hot, but it rains so the trees grow very tall.*

Pages 12–13

Say *A small town is a **village**. Would you like to live in a rainforest village? Why or why not?*

Pages 14–15

Say *Rainforest animals have a lot of plants to eat and water to drink.* Ask *What kind of animals live in rainforests? Yes, lizards and monkeys.*

ESL-ELL tip

Before reading the book, help children understand that both deserts and rainforests are hot. Point to photos on the cover. Demonstrate that both places are hot by wiping your forehead and saying *hot*. Then point to the desert and say *dry*. Point to the rainforest and say *wet*. Encourage children to finish the sentence frame: The desert is hot and ___.

Reading Strategy

Remind children of the skills and strategies when assistance is needed. Say *Stopping at the periods and pausing at the commas will help your reading sound more like natural speech.*

Individual Reading

Have each child read the whole book at his or her own pace while remaining in the group. Observe children as they read. Make note, mentally or in writing, how each child is or is not using the skills and strategies being focused on in this lesson:

1. Are children able to identify and read the reading vocabulary words without assistance?
2. Are children able to pronounce words by segmenting syllables?
3. Are children pausing at commas as they read?
4. Are children able to compare and contrast the information they read?
5. Are children stopping for periods as they read?

3 Text Reading Review

Reading Vocabulary Review

- Have children write vocabulary words on index cards. On the back, have children draw objects that symbolize each word. Have children take turns guessing the word from the drawing.
- Have children highlight, or add, the reading vocabulary words in their copies of *My PM Word Book.* Encourage children to use these words in their writing.

Phonics Review

Write *stem, desert, animals,* and *without* on chart paper. Say the words aloud and enunciate each syllable. Have children say how many syllables each word has. Have them clap with you to verify their answers. Have children say the words slowly first, then faster. Identify syllables on the chart paper: stem, des/ert, an/i/mals, with/out.

Fluency Review

Have children reread page 8. Listen to make sure they are pausing for commas, but not too long. Remind children their reading should sound like they are talking.

Comprehension Review

Have children choose one of the following: plants, people, or animals of the desert and rainforest. Have them fold a sheet of paper in half, draw a picture on each side, and write a phrase or sentence that describes the picture. Remind them that noticing how things are alike and different will help with their reading.

Connection for Writing

Have each child choose which place they would rather live—the desert or the rainforest. Have children write a sentence explaining their preference. They may include an illustration.

Connect to Math

PM Math Readers
Sets of Picture Cards
(Set 15–16)
With children, make picture cards of things, such as desert animals, rainforest animals, and so on. Invite children to compare the members of each set by counting how many cards are in each set, determining which set is the largest, and so on.

4 Assessment and Practice

Reading Vocabulary Application

Provide children with a copy of the Sentence Maker with *tents* written in the top oval. Work with children to create three sentences with the word *tents* and fill in the larger ovals.

Phonics Evaluation

Have children look for words that have more than one syllable. Read the words aloud. Have children clap out the correct number of syllables as you slowly say each word.

Fluency Assessment

Individually, have each child read page 8 to you. Check for smooth reading.

Comprehension Check

Call on volunteers to help complete Venn diagrams that compare and contrast plants, animals, and people who live in the desert and in the rainforest.

Independent Practice

- Have children practice the high-frequency words found within this title using the matching PM High-Frequency Word Cards.
- Provide children with a copy of the activity sheet. Give directions on how to complete the activity sheet. Have children complete the sheet independently.

Differentiated Instruction

- **Kinesthetic** learners can "feel" the story by feeling a cactus you bring to class.
- **Auditory** learners can "hear" the story by listening to an audiotape of rainforest sounds while the teacher reads the book to them.
- **Visual** learners can "see" the story by drawing or painting their own illustrations of deserts or rainforests.

Answer Key

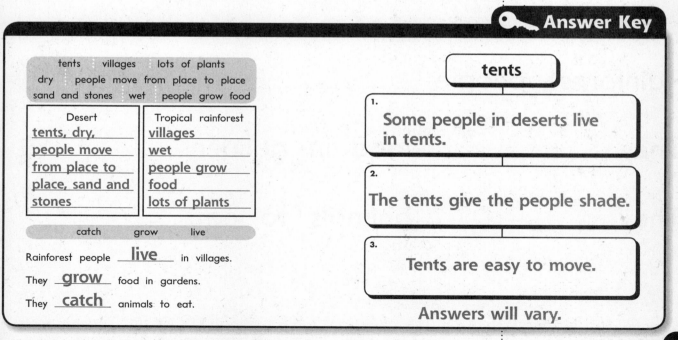

tents	villages	lots of plants
dry	people move from place to place	
sand and stones	wet	people grow food

Desert	Tropical rainforest
tents, dry, people move from place to place, sand and stones	villages wet people grow food lots of plants

catch   grow   live

Rainforest people __live__ in villages.

They __grow__ food in gardens.

They __catch__ animals to eat.

tents

1. Some people in deserts live in tents.

2. The tents give the people shade.

3. Tents are easy to move.

Answers will vary.

Name_____

tents   villages   lots of plants
dry   people move from place to place
sand and stones   wet   people grow food

Desert	Tropical rainforest
_____	_____
_____	_____
_____	_____
_____	_____

catch   grow   live

Rainforest people _____ in villages.

They _____ food in gardens.

They _____ animals to eat.

Life in Hot Places PM Science Readers Teacher's Guide—Green Level

Name_____

Sentence Maker

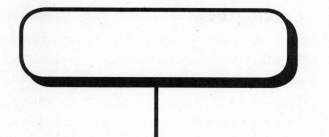

1.

2.

3.

By the Sea

Written by Heather Hammonds

Overview A brother and sister make a journal about their vacation by the sea. They learn about the tides, what's under the sand, and that wind makes waves.

Reading Vocabulary Words vacation p. 2, journal p. 2, tide p. 4, sandworms p. 8

Phonics Skill Demonstrating understanding of plurals

Fluency Point Reading every word without skipping or substituting words

Comprehension Strategy Visualizing information from text, illustrations, diagrams, etc.

Reading Strategy Pointing to each word as you read

Reading Word Count: 251

High-Frequency Words

every   them

time   under

watch   were

1   Before Reading

Build Background

- Introduce the book by reading the title, talking about the cover photograph, and sharing the overview.
- Remind children that pointing to each word can help them read the text. Say *Point to each word as you read it. This helps you to read each word, so you don't skip any.*
- Ask children if anyone has been to the sea or would like to go. Have them discuss what they could do if they were by the sea. Have children share if they have ever been to the sea.

Focus on Reading Vocabulary

- Write each vocabulary word on sheets of paper and read them aloud. Have children draw simple pictures of the vocabulary words. Then ask them to make up sentences using the vocabulary words.
- Model filling in a Same and Opposite chart. Write *sandworms* in the oval. Say *Look at the sandworms on page 9.* Read aloud page 9. In the Same box, write little holes and under the sand. Ask *What are the opposites of* little *and* under? and fill in the Opposite box. (big; on top of, above, over)

Focus on Phonics Understanding plurals

- Write *photos, waves, rocks, footprints, sandworms, holes,* and *surfers* on chart paper. Read the words aloud. Point out that each word ends in *s*. Say *The s at the end of each word means there are more than one.*
- Write *tide, picnic, river,* and *day* on chart paper. Have children tell you how to turn each word into its plural form. Write the plural form by adding *s* to each word, and then use each word in a sentence.

Science Standard:

- **Knows that plants and animals live in a particular habitat**
- **Organisms and environments**

Focus on Fluency

- Read aloud pages 2–3, modeling how you read every word without skipping or substituting a word. Say *I take my time to read each and every word. If I try to read too fast, I might skip a word. When I take my time, it's easier to make sense of words that are new to me.*
- Partner children and have them read pages 2–3. Make sure they are taking the time to read each and every word.

Focus on Comprehension

- Explain that readers can learn a great deal by looking at pictures and by visualizing what they read. Say *As you read, try to make pictures in your head. This will help you make sense of what you read. The drawings and photos will give you information, too.*

2 Reading the Text

Book Talk

Cover   Read aloud the title with children. Point out the author's name. Talk about what surrounds the brother and sister.

Pages 2–3   Say *I see the brother and sister walking in front of a sunny house. I wonder if this is their **vacation** house.* Ask *What does the cover of their journal show you?* (things by the sea; starfish, seashells)

Pages 4–5   Say *Look at their drawing of the beach. Can you see their footprints in the sand? The boy is swimming. It looks like they are having fun!*

Pages 6–7   Say *Wow! The beach sure looks different now. The water is not as high. I wonder if that's because the **tide** is going out.*

Pages 8–9   Say *I'm glad they put a label on this photo of the **sandworms**. I didn't know what they were at first. This is the first time I've seen one.*

Pages 10–11   Say *I see a photo and a drawing.* Ask *What does the photo show? Yes, a river. What does the drawing show? Yes, fish in the river.*

Pages 12–13   Ask *Have you ever seen surfers before? That's one big wave!*

Pages 14–15   Say *Look closely at the picture. Is the family dressed for warm weather or cold weather?* (cold) Ask *What else does the picture tell you about the weather?* (It's cold and raining.) *Is the tide coming in or going out?* (coming in)

ESL-ELL tip

Before reading the book, help children understand that sea and ocean mean the same thing.

- Write *sea* and *see* on chart paper. Say each aloud. Point out the different spellings. Beneath *see*, make an *s* and draw two eyes.
- Remind children that *wave* has two meanings. Point to the photo of the ocean *wave* on pages 10 and 13. Then demonstrate how you *wave* to a friend to say hello.
- For advanced ELL, refer to page 13. Ask *What is another word for watch?* (see, look at)

Reading Strategy

Remind children of the skills and strategies when assistance is needed. Say *As you read, point to each word. Use your finger. This will help you to read each word.*

Individual Reading

Have each child read the whole book at his or her own pace while remaining in the group. Observe children as they read. Make note, mentally or in writing, how each child is or is not using the skills and strategies being focused on in this lesson:

1. Are children able to identify and read the reading vocabulary words without assistance?
2. Are children able to recognize words ending in *s* as the plural form?
3. Are children reading every word without skipping or substituting?
4. Are children visualizing as they read and gleaning information from illustrations or drawings?
5. Are children pointing to each word as they read?

3 Text Reading Review

Reading Vocabulary Review

- Write the vocabulary words on chart paper and have children copy each word onto the lined side of an index card. Have children draw a picture on the back of each index card. Children can combine their cards to play "Go Fish."
- Have children highlight, or add, the reading vocabulary words in their copies of *My PM Word Book*. Encourage children to use these words in their writing.

Phonics Review

Write *vacation, journal, tide,* and *sandworms* on chart paper. Have children say the words aloud. Ask *Which words tell you that there is more than one? Yes,* sandworms. *How do you know? Yes, it ends in* s. Ask *How do you make more than one vacation? Yes, you add* s *to the end of the word.* Write *vacations.* Then ask for volunteers to write the plural form of *journal* and *tide.*

Fluency Review

Have children take turns rereading sections of the book with a partner. Remind children to point to each word as they read.

Comprehension Review

Ask *What was your favorite part of* By the Sea? Say *Draw a picture of something you read that really interested you. Then write two to three sentences about it.*

Connection for Writing

Point out to children that in *By the Sea,* the brother and sister were reporting about each day at the sea. Ask *If you could be with them on one of the days, which day would it be?* Have children review the days with a partner and discuss which day they would pick. Then have each child write a one-day journal telling what the day was like.

Connect to Math

PM Math Readers
The Junior Concert
(Set D/16–17)
Have children imagine that each day ten people come to stay in their house. Ask *How many people would be at the vacation house on day six?* Children can draw stick figures to represent people or come up with their own ways to depict the numbers.

4 Assessment and Practice

Reading Vocabulary Application

Provide children with a copy of the Same and Opposite chart with *tide* written in the oval. Work with children to fill in the Same and Opposite boxes.

Phonics Evaluation

Have children write *photo, wave, rock, footprint, sandworm, hole,* and *surfer* on separate index cards. Have children take turns showing their cards to their partner and asking their partner to write the plural form on the back of the card.

Fluency Assessment

Individually, have each child read a section of the book to you. Listen to see that each child is reading every word without skipping or substituting.

Comprehension Check

Have children look at the picture on page 4. Ask *What color is the water when the sun is out? What color is the sky? Yes, both are blue.* Then refer children to page 15. Ask *What color is the sea on this day? What color is the sky when it's cloudy out? Yes, both are gray.* Say *I wonder if the water in the sea is like a mirror to the sky.*

Independent Practice

- Have children practice the high-frequency words found within this title using the matching PM High-Frequency Word Cards.
- Provide children with a copy of the activity sheet. Give directions on how to complete the activity sheet. Have children complete the sheet independently.

Answer Key

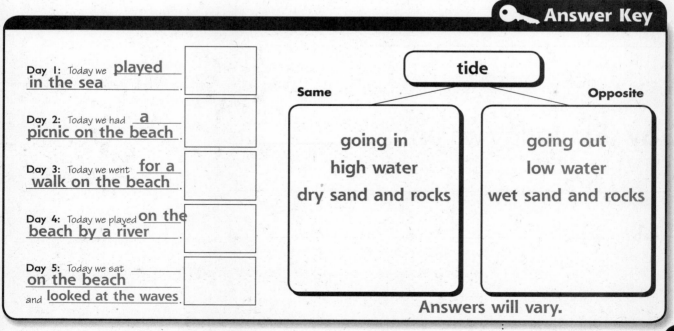

Day 1: Today we **played in the sea** .

Day 2: Today we had **a picnic on the beach** .

Day 3: Today we went **for a walk on the beach** .

Day 4: Today we played **on the beach by a river** .

Day 5: Today we sat **on the beach** and **looked at the waves** .

tide

Same	Opposite
going in high water dry sand and rocks	going out low water wet sand and rocks

Answers will vary.

Name_____

Day 1: Today we _____

_____ .

Day 2: Today we had _____

_____ .

Day 3: Today we went _____

_____ .

Day 4: Today we played _____

_____ .

Day 5: Today we sat _____

_____

and _____ .

Name

Same and Opposite

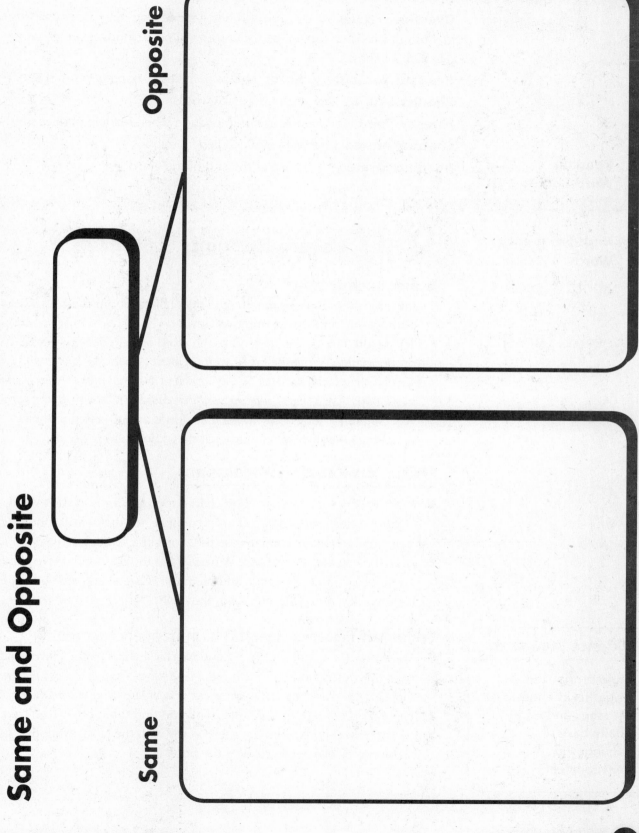

Opposite

Same

Watching Clouds

Written by Julie Haydon

Overview Clouds are described as being made from tiny water droplets or tiny bits of ice. They can tell us about the weather. Clouds might produce rain, hail, or snow.

Reading Vocabulary Words photos p. 5, tiny p. 6, puffy p. 12, shapes p. 15

Phonics Skill Reading high-frequency words

Fluency Point Varying the use of intonation when reading phrases

Comprehension Strategy Making generalizations

Reading Strategy Looking at the end of the word

Reading Word Count: 201

High-Frequency Words

about   soon

ask   tell

every   watch

1   Before Reading

Build Background

- Introduce the book by reading the title, talking about the cover photograph, and sharing the overview.
- Tell children to look at the end of the word to help decide on its pronunciation. Write the word *dark* on chart paper. Say *Look at this word. I see that it ends with the letter "k." What sound does that make? Now I can read the word:* dark. Ask *What is another word that ends in "k"?* (bark, mark, park)
- Ask children if they enjoy looking at clouds and to describe them. Encourage them to talk about what they know about clouds.

Focus on Reading Vocabulary

- Write each vocabulary word on chart paper. Read aloud each word. Have children select one word and give examples for that word. (photos of my dog, tiny feet) Have children use the word in a sentence.
- Model filling in a Word Map. Write *puffy* in the diamond. Have children name objects that are puffy, and fill in the "Give examples!" boxes. Have children describe *puffy,* and fill in the ovals.

Focus on Phonics Reading high-frequency words

- Write *about, ask, every, soon, tell,* and *watch* on chart paper. Have children read the words aloud. Ask *Do you read these words often? Does that make them easy to read?* Say *Seeing these words a lot helps you to read them.*
- Have children look through the book and find three other high-frequency words. Ask children to share their words with the class. Write the words on a chart to display while reading the book.

Science Standard:

- **Knows that the weather changes over seasons and on a daily basis**
- **Changes in environment**

Focus on Fluency

- Say *Some clouds are made of tiny drops of water and tiny bits of ice* (emphasizing "tiny"). Ask *Did you notice how I changed the tone in my voice when I read the word* tiny? *That makes the reading more interesting. Try to change the tone in your voice when you read.*
- Have children practice reading a sentence from the book aloud. Ask them to change the tone of their voices.

Focus on Comprehension

- Explain that after reading a text, readers can make general statements that describe a group of people or things. Have children look at pages 12–13. Say *Look at the clouds. They look different, but what statement can you make about clouds? Right, clouds are in the sky.*

2 Reading the Text

Book Talk

Cover   Read aloud the title with children. Point out the author's name. Ask children to describe the clouds. Ask *Do you like looking at clouds?*

Pages 2–3   Say *These people are outside. What are they doing? Yes, they are watching clouds. Can you describe the clouds? They are big and white.*

Pages 4–5   Say *The boy's mom is working on a* **computer.** *What is she looking at? Yes, it is Earth. Do the clouds she is looking at look different from the clouds on page 4? Yes, they do.*

Pages 6–7   Ask *Do you see how the clouds have different shapes? Sometimes the clouds are low in the sky. What happens when clouds are dark? Yes, it might rain.*

Pages 8–9   Say *These dark clouds are making rain. Is it raining hard or softly on the girl? Yes, it's a hard rain.*

Pages 10–11   Say *I see* **snow** *falling. Where do you think the snow comes from? Right, it falls from clouds. Look at the photo on page 11. That is* **hail.** *Have you ever seen or heard hail fall from the clouds?*

Pages 12–13   Say *I see puffy clouds with the sun shining and dark clouds that look like rain. What can clouds tell us? Yes, they tell us about weather.*

Pages 14–15   Ask *Do you see a familiar shape in the clouds? Yes, it's a fish! Do you ever see shapes of things in clouds?*

ESL-ELL tip

Before reading the book, help children understand that *clouds* tell about weather. Have them draw a picture of clouds on a sunny day and clouds on a rainy day. Label the pictures as "puffy clouds" and "dark clouds." Have them say the words aloud.

Reading Strategy

Remind children of the skills and strategies when assistance is needed. Say *Looking at the letter at the end of the word can tell you what sound it makes. This will help you pronounce unfamiliar words more easily.*

Individual Reading

Have each child read the whole book at his or her own pace while remaining in the group. Observe children as they read. Make note, mentally or in writing, how each child is or is not using the skills and strategies being focused on in this lesson:

1. Are children able to identify and read the reading vocabulary words without assistance?
2. Are children able to read high-frequency words?
3. Are children varying the intonation of their voices when reading phrases?
4. Are children making generalizations while reading?
5. Are children looking at a word's ending sound when reading?

3 Text Reading Review

Reading Vocabulary Review

- Assign vocabulary words to small groups of children. Have them think of words that they associate with the vocabulary words. Help them make a list. Groups can take turns sharing their ideas with the class.
- Have children highlight, or add, the reading vocabulary words in their copies of *My PM Word Book*. Encourage children to use these words in their writing.

Phonics Review

Have children look at the chart of high-frequency words you have displayed. Have them write the words on flash cards. Allow children to work with a partner and play a game. The team who can read the most cards without errors is the winner.

Fluency Review

Have children reread the book in pairs. Partners can alternate reading pages. Have children record their readings. Remind them to use their voices to make their recordings interesting.

Comprehension Review

Have children reread the book in pairs. Have partners decide on one statement that can be said of all clouds. Share their generalizations with the class.

Connection for Writing

Have each child draw a picture of clouds. Have him or her write a list, using words from the book that describe the picture. Encourage each child to use some of the words from the book.

Connect to Math

PM Math Readers
Lucy's Garden (Set 15–16)
With children, make a weather report for Lucy's garden. Invite children to say how many clouds are in the sky and to describe them. As the day progresses, they should tell how many more (or fewer) clouds are in the sky and what kind of weather they will produce.

4 Assessment and Practice

Reading Vocabulary Application

Provide children with a copy of the Word Map with *tiny* in the diamond. Work with children to find examples of their word to fill in the boxes. Have children think of words that describe *tiny* and fill in the ovals.

Phonics Evaluation

Write the following words on flash cards: *about, ask, every, soon, tell, watch.* Individually, have each child read the flash cards aloud. Show the cards slowly at first, then increase the speed.

Fluency Assessment

Individually, have each child read pages 10–13. Listen to make sure children are varying their intonation.

Comprehension Check

Individually, have each child make a generalization about clouds.

Independent Practice

- Have children practice the high-frequency words found within this title using the matching PM High-Frequency Word Cards.
- Provide children with a copy of the activity sheet. Have children use a key word to write a sentence for each illustration. Have children complete the sheet independently.

Differentiated Instruction

- **Kinesthetic** learners can "feel" the story by creating clouds with cotton balls on drawing paper.
- **Auditory** learners can "hear" the story by listening to someone else reading the book to them.
- **Visual** learners can "see" the story by drawing their own shapes of clouds.

Answer Key

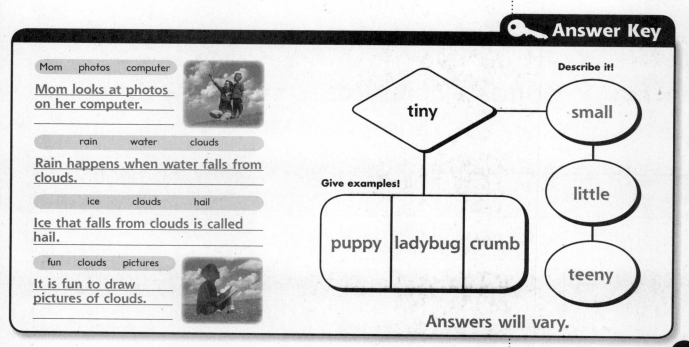

| Mom | photos | computer |

Mom looks at photos on her computer.

| rain | water | clouds |

Rain happens when water falls from clouds.

| ice | clouds | hail |

Ice that falls from clouds is called hail.

| fun | clouds | pictures |

It is fun to draw pictures of clouds.

Describe it!

tiny — small

Give examples!

puppy | ladybug | crumb

little

teeny

Answers will vary.

Name_____

Mom   photos   computer

_____

_____

_____

rain   water   clouds

_____

_____

_____

ice   clouds   hail

_____

_____

_____

fun   clouds   pictures

_____

_____

_____

Name _____

Word Map

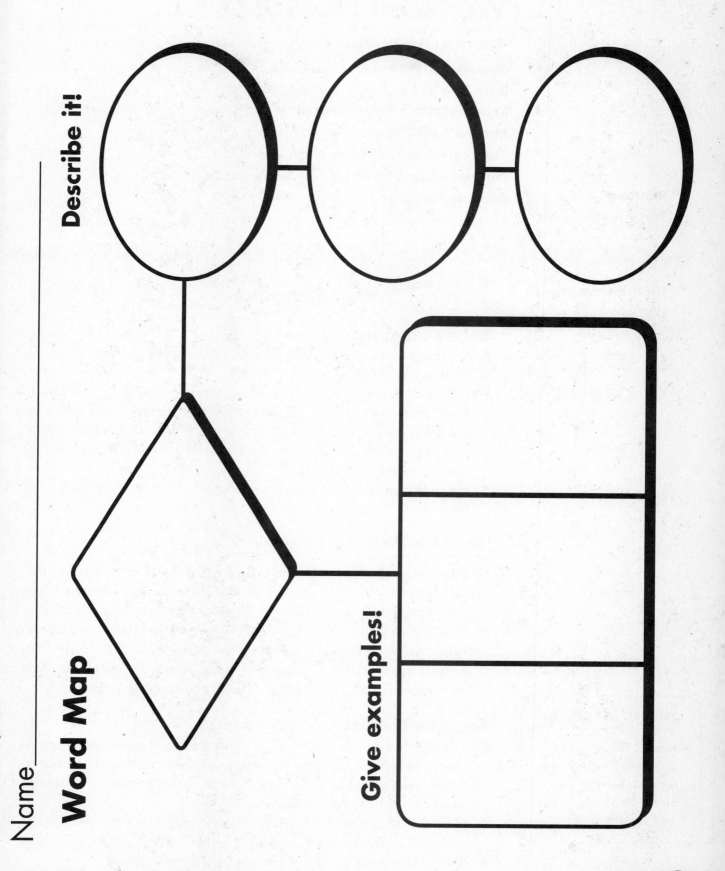

Describe it!

Give examples!

We Need the Sun

Written by Heather Hammonds

Overview The sun is important to life on Earth. It gives us heat and light. Some times of the year are warmer than others.

Reading Vocabulary Words daytime p. 4, autumn p. 8, nighttime p. 14

Phonics Skill Compound words

Fluency Point Reading smoothly

Comprehension Strategy Connecting text-to-self

Reading Strategy Checking for a pattern

Reading Word Count: 202

High-Frequency Words

end	live
every	warm
grow	when

1 Before Reading

Build Background

- Introduce the book by reading the title, talking about the cover photograph, and sharing the overview.
- Explain to children that as they read the text, they should think of how the story connects to their life. Say *This book is about the sun.* Ask *How does the sun affect you? Do you prefer sunny days or cloudy days? Do you like nighttime or daytime better? Making a connection to the book will help you understand what you are reading.*
- Have children share what they know about the sun. Ask them to describe the sun.

Focus on Reading Vocabulary

- Write *autumn* on chart paper. Read the word aloud. Have children use the word in a sentence. Next, write *daytime* and *nighttime*. Read the words aloud. Ask *How are these words similar? Yes, they both have the word* time *in them.*
- Model filling in a Word Sorter. Write *daytime* in the top box. Have children name two words that are different for the next level, such as *animals* and *people*. The lower three boxes will have examples of daytime animals (cows, dogs, birds) and daytime people (children, mail carrier, bus driver).

Focus on Phonics Compound words

- Write *sun/rise* on chart paper. Explain that some words are made from two words. Readers can divide compound words into smaller, familiar words to help read these long words. Ask children to name another compound word with the word *sun* (*sunset*).
- Have children suggest three other compound words with *sun*. Write each suggested word on the chart. (*sunshine, sunburn, suntan, sunflower*) Draw a line to show the division of the words.

Science Standard:

- **Knows that the sun provides heat and light to Earth**
- **Light, heat, electricity, and magnetism**

Focus on Fluency

- Read page 2 aloud. First, read with unnatural interruptions. Ask *Was I reading smoothly?* Say *Reading smoothly helps you understand better.* Read page 2 in a natural manner. Ask *How was that better?*
- Have children select a page from the book. Have them read to a partner to see if they are reading smoothly. Have children practice until their reading is smooth.

Focus on Comprehension

- Explain that every reader can connect what he or she reads to his or her own experiences. Have children look at pages 4–5. Ask *Do you like getting up in the morning? Do you like to get up at sunrise or later in the day?* Have children look at pages 6 and 9. Ask *Which of these activities do you prefer? Why? Do you like to be in the sunshine or indoors? Why?*

2 Reading the Text

Book Talk

Cover

Read aloud the title with children. Point out the author's name. Talk about how hot the sun looks and the colors of the sunset.

Pages 2–3

Say *I am noticing how big the sun is compared to **Earth**. What does the sun give us? Yes, it gives us light and warmth.*

Pages 4–5

Ask *What is the boy doing? Yes, he is waking up. It is daytime. What other animals get up at **sunrise**?*

Pages 6–7

Say *I see a beach with people. What time of year is it? Yes, it's summer. How does the sun feel in the summer? Yes, it's hot.*

Pages 8–9

Say *I am noticing other seasons. This pattern of giving information helps me with my reading. In which season does it snow?*

Pages 10–11

Say *This picture shows plants that are getting a lot of sun. What compound word do you see that describes the sun? Yes, sunshine. The sun is shining on the garden.*

Pages 12–13

Ask *What kind of place is this? Yes, a desert. There is not much growing there. Do you think it is hot there all the time?*

Pages 14–15

Say *The sun is setting. What time of day is it? Yes, it will be nighttime. What do you do at nighttime?*

Reading Strategy

Remind children of the skills and strategies when assistance is needed. Say *Sometimes you will see repeated words or phrases that form patterns. Check for patterns as you read.*

Individual Reading

Have each child read the whole book at his or her own pace while remaining in the group. Observe children as they read. Make note, mentally or in writing, how each child is or is not using the skills and strategies being focused on in this lesson:

1. Are children able to identify and read the reading vocabulary words without assistance?
2. Are children able to identify and read compound words?
3. Are children reading smoothly to improve comprehension?
4. Are children making text-to-self connections while reading?
5. Are children checking for patterns when reading?

3 Text Reading Review

Reading Vocabulary Review

- Have children draw a daytime scene and a nighttime scene on different sheets of paper. Have them label their drawings. Share the drawings with the class and have children say the corresponding words.
- Have children highlight, or add, the reading vocabulary words in their copies of *My PM Word Book*. Encourage children to use these words in their writing.

Phonics Review

Write *sometimes* on chart paper. Have children say the two smaller words and write them on chart paper: *some* + *times*. Add the following words: *sunrise, daytime, sunshine, nighttime, sunset*. Have children write the two words as you did on their own paper. Write the correct divisions on the chart paper.

Fluency Review

Have children reread several pages from the book with a partner. Remind children to read smoothly. Encourage children to practice reading the same pages until they are reading as though they were talking.

Connect to Math

PM Math Readers

Making a Clock Cake
(Set 17–18)
With children, draw a clock cake that represents the time the sun rises and sets. Use a computer to find out exact times for your area.

Comprehension Review

Have children reread the book in pairs. Have partners share if they prefer daytime, with the sun out, or nighttime. Remind children that making connections between themselves and the text helps with their reading.

Connection for Writing

Have each child create a visual chart for each season. Have him or her write a phrase, using the same pattern as in the book, that describes how much sun Earth is getting.

4 Assessment and Practice

Reading Vocabulary Application

Provide children with a Word Sorter with the word *nighttime* in the top box. Work with children to name two activities they do at nighttime in the next level of boxes. Have children describe each activity on the appropriate side of the organizer.

Phonics Evaluation

Write *night, day, snow,* and *rain* on chart paper. With children, brainstorm a list of compound words that begin with these words. Ask volunteers to provide a sentence with a word from the list.

Fluency Assessment

Individually, have each child read the story to you. Check for smooth reading.

Comprehension Check

Individually, have each child share which season he or she prefers and why.

Independent Practice

- Have children practice the high-frequency words found within this title using the matching PM High-Frequency Word Cards.
- Provide children with a copy of the activity sheet. Give directions on how to complete the activity sheet. Have children complete the sheet independently.

Differentiated Instruction

- **Kinesthetic** learners can "feel" the story by stepping outside to feel the sun and providing the class with a weather report.
- **Auditory** learners can "hear" the story by listening to songs about sunny days or rainy days.
- **Visual** learners can "see" the story by drawing illustrations that show how the sun heats and lights Earth.

🔑 Answer Key

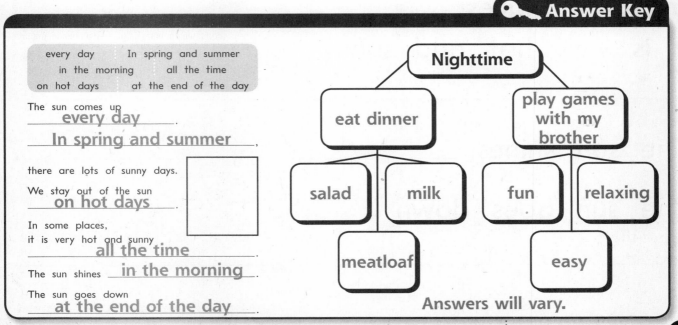

every day	In spring and summer
in the morning	all the time
on hot days	at the end of the day

The sun comes up ___every day___.

___In spring and summer___,

there are lots of sunny days.
We stay out of the sun
___on hot days___.

In some places,
it is very hot and sunny
___all the time___.
The sun shines ___in the morning___.

The sun goes down
___at the end of the day___.

Nighttime

eat dinner

play games with my brother

salad   milk   fun   relaxing

meatloaf   easy

Answers will vary.

Name_____

The sun comes up

_____.

_____,

there are lots of sunny days.

We stay out of the sun

_____.

In some places,
it is very hot and sunny

_____.

The sun shines _____.

The sun goes down

_____.

Name

Word Sorter

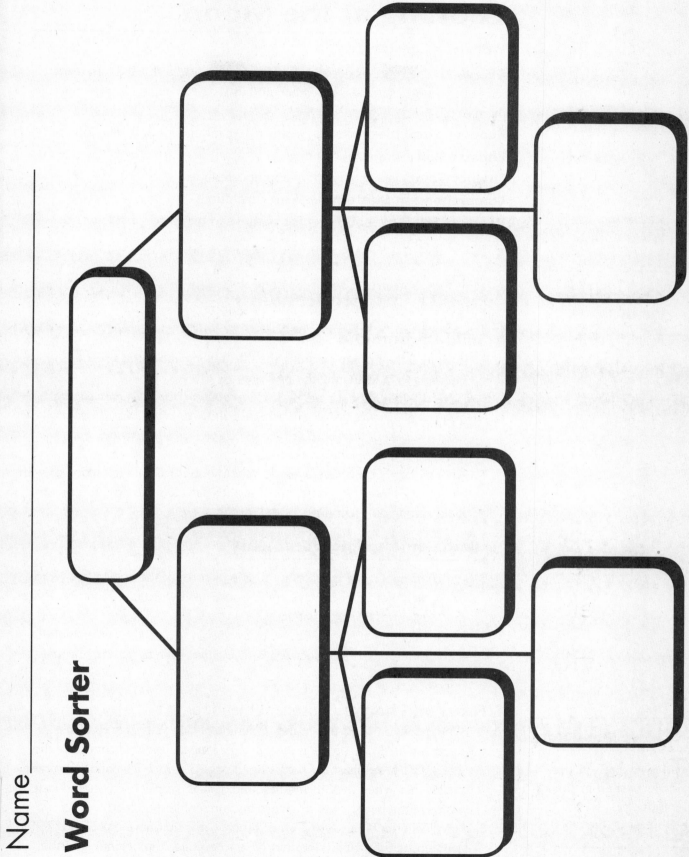

Looking at the Moon

Written by Julie Haydon

Overview The moon is described and compared to Earth. Children learn about the moon's surface, its weather, and its shapes. People have been to the moon.

Reading Vocabulary Words weather p. 6, mountains p. 8, telescope p. 14

Phonics Skill Consonant blend: *pl*

Fluency Point Taking a breath at appropriate times

Comprehension Strategy Drawing conclusions

Reading Strategy Looking at the picture and the word's first letter

Reading Word Count: 228

High-Frequency Words

could	same
far	some
need	very

1 Before Reading

Build Background

- Introduce the book by reading the title, talking about the cover photograph, and sharing the overview.
- Have children look at page 4. Say *A picture can help you figure out the meaning of a word.* Ask *Do you recognize the large planet? Yes, it is Earth. What is the first letter of the word? Yes, "E." When you read, use pictures and a word's first letter to read unfamiliar words.*
- Ask children if they have ever seen the moon through a telescope or with binoculars. Have them describe what they saw. Discuss how the moon looks during different times of the month.

Focus on Reading Vocabulary

- On chart paper, write and draw simple pictures of the vocabulary words. Read each word aloud. Have children use each word in a sentence. Write their responses on chart paper.
- Model filling in a Word Web. Write *weather* in the center. Have children name different words associated with *weather*, such as *hot, cold,* or *rainy,* and fill in the ovals.

Focus on Phonics Consonant blend: *pl*

- Write *plants* on chart paper and underline *pl*. Say Plants *begins with a consonant* pl *blend. A blend is the* p *and the* l *sound together.* Pronounce the word slowly, emphasizing the *pl*. Read page 5 aloud. Tell children to raise their hands when they hear a *pl* sound. *(plants, people)* Have them locate the word on the page. Write the word and underline the blend.
- Have children brainstorm a list of other words that have a *pl* blend. Remind children that the blend does not have to occur at the beginning of the word. *(please, place, plate, purple, maple)*

Science Standard:

- **Knows some of the objects seen in the night sky**
- **Objects in the sky**

Focus on Fluency

- Have children look at page 5. Say *There is a lot of text on this page. I need to take breaths at the right time.* Read the page aloud. First, rush through the sentences without breathing. Then, model breathing at appropriate times.
- Ask for volunteers to read the same page. Remind children not to exaggerate their breathing and to pause at periods.

Focus on Comprehension

- Explain that readers can combine what they read with their experience to figure out more than what the author says. To draw a conclusion, have children look at page 5. Read the text aloud. Ask *The author doesn't tell us, but do you think you would see dogs, people, and trees on the moon? Why not? Right, the moon does not have water or air.*

2　Reading the Text

Book Talk

Cover　　Read aloud the title with children. Point out the author's name. Talk about how a telescope can help people see the moon better.

Pages 2–3　Say *The moon is easy to see at night. Sometimes it looks so big that you could touch it. Have you ever seen the moon during the day?*

Pages 4–5　Say *Look at the moon and Earth. Which one is bigger? Earth has people, animals, and plants. What do you think is on the moon?*

Pages 6–7　Say *The children are wearing coats. What is the weather like? Yes, it looks a little cool. What other kind of weather do we have on Earth? Yes, sometimes it is hot.*

Pages 8–9　Say *These pictures of the moon make it look cold and empty. What kind of features do you notice? Yes, I see mountains and holes, too.*

Pages 10–11　Say *These pictures show the different shapes of the moon. Have you ever watched the night sky to see the moon get bigger or smaller?*

Pages 12–13　Ask *Where is that man? Yes, he is on the moon! He is an astronaut. Would you like to make a trip to the moon? Why or why not?*

Pages 14–15　Say *This boy is using a telescope. Do you know what a telescope does? Yes, it makes the moon look bigger.*

ESL-ELL tip

Before reading the book, have children share the words in their culture or family for *moon*. Have the class repeat these words, along with their English equivalents. Show how some words, such as *luna*, have a related English word: *lunar, lunar landing.*

Reading Strategy

Remind children of the skills and strategies when assistance is needed. Say *By looking at the picture and at a word's first letter, you can figure out some unfamiliar words.*

Individual Reading

Have each child read the whole book at his or her own pace while remaining in the group. Observe children as they read. Make note, mentally or in writing, how each child is or is not using the skills and strategies being focused on in this lesson:

1. Are children able to identify and read the reading vocabulary words without assistance?
2. Are children able to pronounce words with consonant blend *pl*?
3. Are children taking breaths at appropriate times?
4. Are children drawing conclusions while reading?
5. Are children looking at the picture and the word's first letter when reading?

3   Text Reading Review

Reading Vocabulary Review

- Have children write *mountains* at the top of a sheet of paper. Read aloud. On the bottom of their paper, have children draw mountains they would see on Earth or mountains they would see on the moon.
- Have children highlight, or add, the reading vocabulary words in their copies of *My PM Word Book*. Encourage children to use these words in their writing.

Phonics Review

Write *plow* on chart paper. Have children find a word in the book that has a *pl* blend (*plants, people*). Add to the chart paper. Have children brainstorm three other words with the *pl* blend. Ask children to practice saying the words aloud.

Fluency Review

Have children reread the book in groups. Members can alternate reading pages. Listen to see if children are taking breaths at appropriate times. Model correct breathing, if necessary.

Comprehension Review

Have children look at the photo on page 12. Ask *Why do you think the man is wearing a spacesuit?* Write responses on chart paper. Review conclusions and reach one as a class: *There is no air for him to breathe.*

Connection for Writing

Have each child write a list of words or phrases from the book that describe the moon. Have him or her choose four favorite words or phrases. Ask each child to draw a moon and write the four words inside.

Connect to Math

PM Math Readers
The Class Photograph
(Set 17–18)
With children, look at photographs of the nine planets. Make a class graph of the planets, from smallest to largest. Invite children to color and label the planets.

4 Assessment and Practice

Reading Vocabulary Application

Provide children with a copy of the Word Web with the word *telescope* in the center. Work with children to write different words associated with *telescope* and fill in the ovals.

Phonics Evaluation

Write *plants, people, please,* and *maple* on index cards. Individually, have each child read the words aloud.

Fluency Assessment

Individually, have each child read several pages for you. Make sure children are breathing at appropriate times.

Comprehension Check

Individually, have each child look at the photo on page 13 and tell why he or she thinks Earth looks blue.

Independent Practice

- Have children practice the high-frequency words found within this title using the matching PM High-Frequency Word Cards.
- Provide children with a copy of the activity sheet. Have children complete each sentence with one of the "ee" words. For the true or false statements, have children use a check mark if true and an x if false.

Answer Key

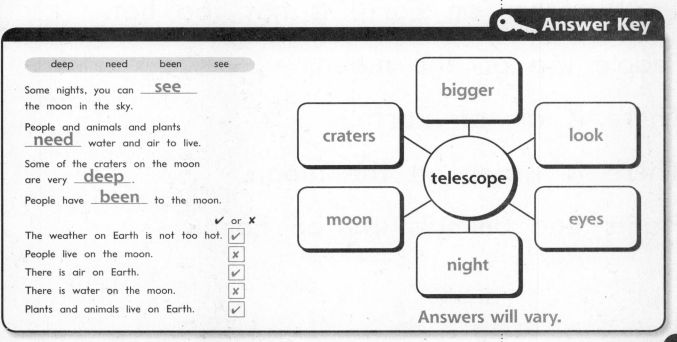

deep	need	been	see

Some nights, you can ___**see**___ the moon in the sky.

People and animals and plants ___**need**___ water and air to live.

Some of the craters on the moon are very ___**deep**___.

People have ___**been**___ to the moon.

✔ or ✗

The weather on Earth is not too hot.	✔
People live on the moon.	✗
There is air on Earth.	✔
There is water on the moon.	✗
Plants and animals live on Earth.	✔

Word Web: telescope — bigger, craters, look, moon, eyes, night

Answers will vary.

Name_____

Some nights, you can _____ the moon in the sky.

People and animals and plants _____ water and air to live.

Some of the craters on the moon are very _____.

People have _____ to the moon.

✔ or ✗

The weather on Earth is not too hot. ☐

People live on the moon. ☐

There is air on Earth. ☐

There is water on the moon. ☐

Plants and animals live on Earth. ☐

Name _____

Word Web

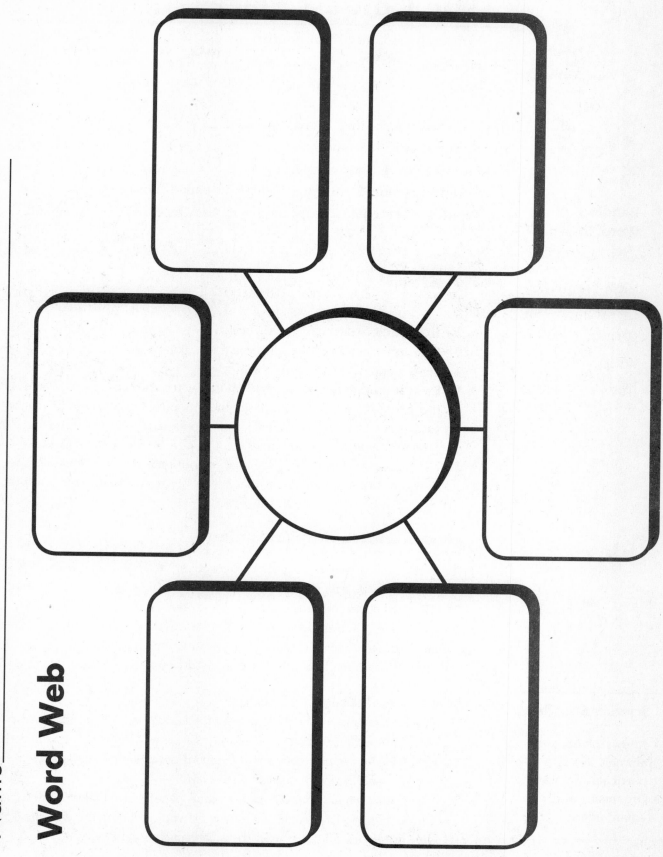

The Coldest Places

Written by Heather Hammonds

Overview The Antarctic and Arctic are two of the coldest places. Mountains are cold, too. Animals live on land and in the sea. People stay warm inside.

Reading Vocabulary Words clothes p. 2, swims p. 7, thick p. 11

Phonics Skill Root words

Fluency Point Using strategies to pronounce unknown words

Comprehension Strategy Building background knowledge

Reading Strategy Getting your mouth ready for the first letter's sound

Reading Word Count: 224

High-Frequency Words

grow   their

keep   them

live   warm

<hr>

Science Standard:

- **Knows plants and animals live in a particular habitat**
- **Organisms and environment**

1 Before Reading

Build Background

- Introduce the book by reading the title, talking about the cover photograph, and sharing the overview.
- Look at page 4. Explain to children that when they come to a word they don't know, they need to get their mouths ready for the first letter's sound. Point out *Antarctic.* Form your mouth for the first letter's sound /a/. Pronounce *Antarctic,* emphasizing /a/.
- Have children share what they know about cold places. Ask children to describe some of the animals that live in very cold places. Encourage them to discuss how the animals stay warm.

Focus on Reading Vocabulary

- Write each vocabulary word on chart paper. Read aloud each word. Ask *What do we do with* clothes? *What animal* swims? *Name an animal with* thick *fur*. Have children use each word in a sentence.
- Model filling in a Same and Opposite chart. Write *clothes* in the oval. Have children name words that are the same as clothes and fill in the Same side. Have children name words that animals have that are the opposite of clothes.

Focus on Phonics Root words

- Write *coldest* and *windy* on chart paper. Discuss that new words can be formed when an ending is added. Say *If you don't know the meaning of the new word, look for the root word. If I drop the endings that I underlined, I can see the roots:* cold *and* wind. *I know those words.*
- Write *places, houses,* and *warmest* on chart paper. Have children write the words on paper and circle the root word and underline the ending. When they finish, discuss the correct roots: *place, house, warm.*

Focus on Fluency

- Write *Antarctic* and *icebergs* on chart paper. Say *These are not familiar words. I can try to sound out each syllable and look for familiar patterns.* Segment the syllables on chart paper, then pronounce the words syllable by syllable. Read each word clearly.
- Have children select and read a page in the book. Ask them to use several strategies to pronounce unknown words.

Focus on Comprehension

- Explain that readers use their knowledge about a subject to figure out what a book is about. Have children look at the title and pictures. Ask *What do you know about cold places? What do you know about polar bears and whales?* Encourage children to share their knowledge.

2   Reading the Text

Book Talk

Cover   Read aloud the title with children. Point out the author's name. Talk about the kinds of animals that live in such cold places.

Pages 2–3   Say *When it is cold outside, we wear warm clothes. What do people do if they live in a place where it is cold all of the time?*

Pages 4–5   Ask *What kind of animals are these? Yes, they are penguins. Remember to use pictures to help you pronounce unknown words.*

Pages 6–7   Say *I see that the bear is the same color as the ice. Do you think the water is cold? How does the polar bear stay warm? Yes, its thick fur.*

Pages 8–9   Say *In this picture, I see green, but no trees. What kind of animals are lying on the rocks? Yes, seals. Do you think the rocks keep them warm? What else keeps them warm? Yes, their blubber!*

Pages 10–11 Say *In this picture the tall **mountains** have snow on them. Look at that animal. What does it look like? Yes, it has horns, fur, and a hump.*

Pages 12–13 Say *This place looks very cold. The river has turned to ice.* Ask *What kind of animals like to swim in cold water? Yes, whales and seals.*

Pages 14–15 Say *Some people must live in cold places. What can they do to stay warm? Yes, they can wear warm clothes or stay inside.*

Reading Strategy

Remind children of the skills and strategies when assistance is needed. Say *Looking at the first letter of the word and getting your mouth ready to make the sound will help you read an unknown word.*

Individual Reading

Have each child read the whole book at his or her own pace while remaining in the group. Observe children as they read. Make note, mentally or in writing, how each child is or is not using the skills and strategies being focused on in this lesson:

1. Are children able to identify and read the reading vocabulary words without assistance?
2. Are children able to find root words to pronounce new words?
3. Are children using different strategies to pronounce unknown words?
4. Are children activating background knowledge while reading?
5. Are children getting their mouths ready for the first letter's sound?

3 Text Reading Review

Reading Vocabulary Review

- Have children draw a picture of a polar bear, yak, whale, or seal. Have them add a sentence to their drawing, using either the word *thick* or *swims*.
- Have children highlight, or add, the reading vocabulary words in their copies of *My PM Word Book*. Encourage children to use these words in their writing.

Phonics Review

Write *clothes, called,* and *islands* on chart paper. Have children tell you the roots. Ask *What endings do you see on these words?* Underline the endings. Ask *What are the roots?* Circle the correct roots. Have children provide other words that end in *s* from the book, such as *days, places,* and *penguins,* and write the words on the chart paper.

Fluency Review

Have children read sections of the book to a partner. Children should attempt to read all words. Remind children to use several strategies to pronounce unknown words. Encourage partners to assist but not to "tell" the word.

Comprehension Review

Have children share one fact of information they know about cold places or animals with the class. Write their responses on chart paper.

Connection for Writing

Have each child write a journal entry. Say *Today we visited the coldest places by reading the book. I want you to write a journal page about the coldest places. Describe three things you see while you are there.*

Connect to Math

PM Math Readers
Billy, the Number Champ
(Set 16–17)
With children, count the penguins on page 5. (11) Ask them to determine how many penguins there would be in line to dive if 3 more joined the line. $(11 + 3 = 14)$

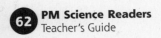

4 Assessment and Practice

Reading Vocabulary Application

Provide children with a copy of a Same and Opposite chart with *thick* written in the top oval. Work with children to write words similar to *thick* on the left side and words opposite of *thick* on the right side.

Phonics Evaluation

Write *islands, grows, moved, called, coldest, warmest, windy,* and *lucky* on separate index cards. Mix the cards up. Individually, have each child tell you the root words.

Fluency Assessment

Individually, have each child read the story to you. Check that children are using different strategies to pronounce unfamiliar words.

Comprehension Check

Individually, have each child share a fact he or she knew about cold places before reading the book.

Independent Practice

- Have children practice the high-frequency words found within this title using the matching PM High-Frequency Word Cards.
- Provide children with a copy of the activity sheet. Give directions on how to complete the activity sheet. Have children complete the sheet independently.

Differentiated Instruction

- **Kinesthetic** learners can "feel" the story by creating an icescape in a shallow bowl.
- **Auditory** learners can "hear" the story by listening to someone else reading the book to them.
- **Visual** learners can "see" the story by painting their own illustrations of cold places.

Answer Key

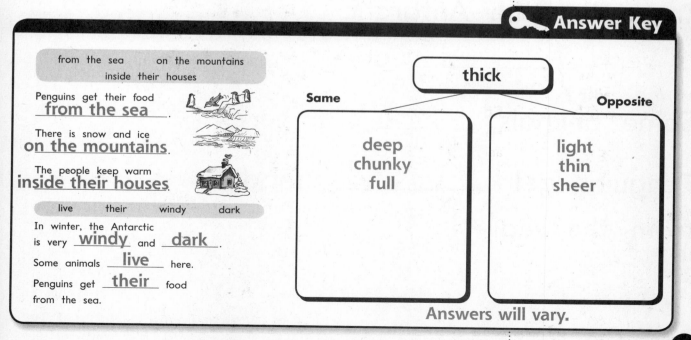

Answers will vary.

Name_____

from the sea   on the mountains
inside their houses

Penguins get their food

_____.

There is snow and ice

_____.

The people keep warm

_____.

live   their   windy   dark

In winter, the Antarctic
is very _____ and _____.

Some animals _____ here.

Penguins get _____ food
from the sea.

Name

Same and Opposite

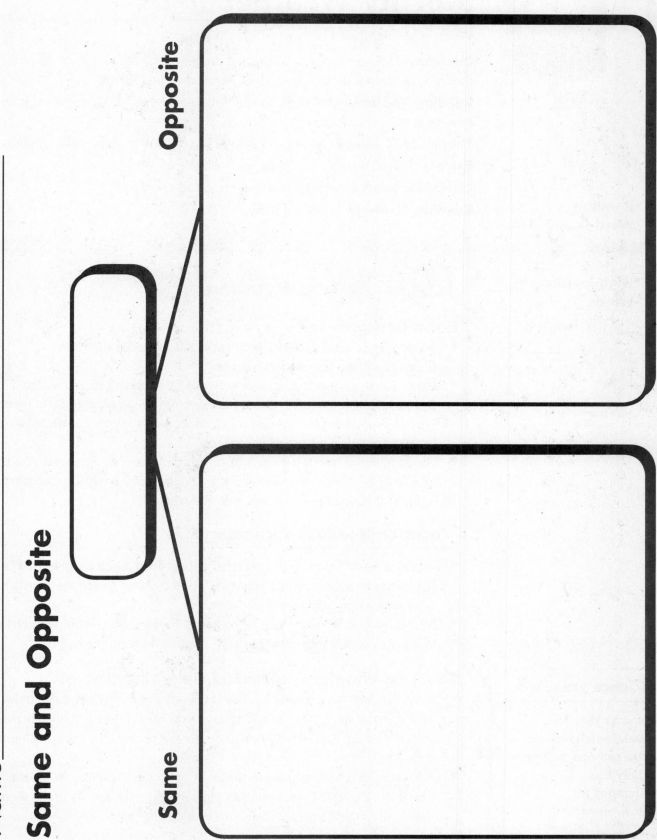

Opposite

Same

Stormy Weather

Written by Heather Hammonds

Overview Different types of storms are described. Children learn about snowstorms, thunderstorms, tornadoes, hurricanes, and floods.

Reading Vocabulary Words stormy (title), computer p. 3, dangerous p. 5, thunder p. 6

Phonics Skill Using knowledge of syllables to decode multiple-syllable words

Fluency Point Voice falling at the end of declarative sentences

Comprehension Strategy Recognizing cause and effect

 Reading Strategy Sounding it out

Reading Word Count: 208

High-Frequency Words

about	much
fall	start
how	turn

Science Standard:

- **Knows that the weather changes over the seasons and on a daily basis**
- **Changes in environment**

---

1 Before Reading

Build Background

- Introduce the book by reading the title, talking about the cover photograph, and sharing the overview.
- Explain that readers can learn new words by sounding them out. Say *If you see an unfamiliar word, look at the letters. Say the letters from left to right. Try to read the word by sounding out all the letters. Decide if it sounds like a more familiar word, then try to read it again.*
- Have children share what kinds of storms they have experienced. Ask them to give details. For example, ask if it was rainy, cold, or windy. Encourage them to describe the event and how they felt.

Focus on Reading Vocabulary

- Write each vocabulary word on chart paper. Read aloud each word. Have children use each word in a sentence. Have children select one word and write an exciting sentence about a storm.
- Model filling in a Word Web. Write *stormy* in the center. Work with children to think of words they associate with *stormy* and fill in the ovals.

Focus on Phonics Decoding multiple-syllable words

- Write *hurricane* on chart paper. Say the word aloud, first normally, then slowly. Ask children to clap with you as you read it slowly. Ask *How many times did we clap? Yes, three.* Show them where to segment the syllables and write *hur/ri/cane*.
- Add *snowstorm* and *lightning* to the chart paper. Ask children to say the words aloud and tell you where to segment the syllables. Write the words again, correctly segmented: *snow/storm* and *light/ning*.

Focus on Fluency

- Have children look at pages 2–3. Point out the periods. Say *When you read aloud, you want to drop your voice at the end of a sentence that ends with a period.*
- Read pages 2–3 aloud, modeling how the voice falls at the end of a declarative sentence. Ask volunteers to read page 4 aloud.

Focus on Comprehension

- Explain that active readers look for cause-and-effect relationships during reading. Have children look at pages 8–9. Say *This photo shows a tornado. The tornado is an event. What effect does the tornado cause? Yes, it causes houses and trees to fall down.* Have children describe other effects of storms.

2 Reading the Text

Book Talk

Cover   Read aloud the title with children. Point out the author's name. Talk about the tornado and lightning.

Pages 2–3   Ask *Why are these children inside? Yes, it's raining. What are they looking at on the computer? Yes, it looks like a map.*

Pages 4–5   Ask *What kind of storm is this? Yes, it's a snowstorm.* Say *Look at the photo. Why is it dangerous to go out? Yes, it's windy and cold!*

Pages 6–7   Say *This **lightning** looks dangerous, too. Do you know why? Yes, it is dangerous if it strikes you. What happens after you see lightning? Yes, you usually hear thunder after lightning.*

Pages 8–9   Say *I see a **tornado**. This storm touches the ground. What kind of effect do tornadoes have? Yes, they can completely damage a house.*

Pages 10–11   Say *This photo is taken from space. It shows how big this **hurricane** is. What happens during a hurricane? Yes, it rains and the wind blows.*

Pages 12–13   Say *These people are looking at water covering a street. What do you think happened? Yes, it rained too much and **flooded** the streets.*

Pages 14–15   Say *The man is using computers and balloons to find out about the weather. What will he do with this information? Yes, he will tell people so they can prepare for bad weather.*

ESL-ELL tip

Before reading the book, help children understand that there are different types of storms. Use the table of contents to show them the words *Snowstorms* and *Thunderstorms.* Show them a picture of each type of storm and discuss the elements of these storms. Help children associate features with each type of storm. Have them prepare their own flash cards for each word.

Reading Strategy

Remind children of the skills and strategies when assistance is needed. Say *When you see a difficult word, try to sound it out. Say the letters from left to right. Say the sounds aloud and try to read the word.*

Individual Reading

Have each child read the whole book at his or her own pace while remaining in the group. Observe children as they read. Make note, mentally or in writing, how each child is or is not using the skills and strategies being focused on in this lesson:

1. Are children able to identify and read the reading vocabulary words without assistance?
2. Are children able to use knowledge of syllables to decode multiple-syllable words?
3. Are children making their voices fall at the end of declarative sentences?
4. Are children recognizing cause-and-effect relationships while reading?
5. Are children sounding out letters when reading?

3 Text Reading Review

Reading Vocabulary Review

- Have children fold a sheet of paper in fourths and draw a storyboard about a storm. Under each frame, have them write a sentence using at least two of the following words: *stormy, computer, dangerous, thunder.*
- Have children highlight, or add, the reading vocabulary words in their copies of *My PM Word Book*. Encourage children to use these words in their writing.

Phonics Review

Write *tornadoes* and *hurricane* on chart paper. Have children say the words aloud and clap as they say each word. Ask *How many syllables does each word have? Yes, three.* Have children correctly segment the words (tor/na/does, hur/ri/cane).

Fluency Review

Have children take turns rereading pages to a partner. Remind children to drop their voices at the end of a sentence. This helps readers follow the story.

Comprehension Review

Have children select one type of storm. Have them get in similar groups and talk about the effects their storm has on people and on the environment. Encourage children to draw from personal experiences and the book.

Connection for Writing

Have each child create a weather warning about a storm. Have each child choose a storm, brainstorm a list of dangerous elements, then write a few sentences that warn people about the approaching storm.

Connect to Math

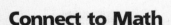

PM Math Readers
The Secret Message
(Set 17–18)
With children, play the secret message game, using vocabulary words from the book (e.g., *thunderstorm*). Write the code on the board.

4 Assessment and Practice

Reading Vocabulary Application

Provide children with a copy of the Word Web with *thunder* written in the center. Work with children to write different words associated with thunder and fill in the ovals.

Phonics Evaluation

On blank cards write the words *snowstorm, lightning, tornadoes,* and *hurricane.* Individually, have each child rewrite the words, showing the syllable breaks. You may add *thunderstorm* as a bonus word.

Fluency Assessment

Individually, have each child read the story to you. Listen for the child to drop his or her voice at the end of a sentence.

Comprehension Check

Individually, have each child explain what effect or effects certain types of storms have on people or buildings.

Independent Practice

- Have children practice the high-frequency words found within this title using the matching PM High-Frequency Word Cards.
- Provide children with a copy of the activity sheet. Give directions on how to complete the activity sheet. Have children complete the sheet independently.

Differentiated Instruction

- **Kinesthetic** learners can "feel" the story by using a computer to find a weather forecast.
- **Auditory** learners can "hear" the story by listening to someone else reading the book to them.
- **Visual** learners can "see" the story by drawing different illustrations of each type of storm mentioned in the book.

Answer Key

computer	storm	weather
lightning	tornadoes	rain

1 syllable	2 syllables	3 syllables
storm	lightning	computer
rain	weather	tornadoes

blow   blows

The wind __blows__ fast inside a tornado.

Tornadoes can __blow__ trees and houses down.

In a cyclone the wind __blows__ hard, and lots of rain falls.

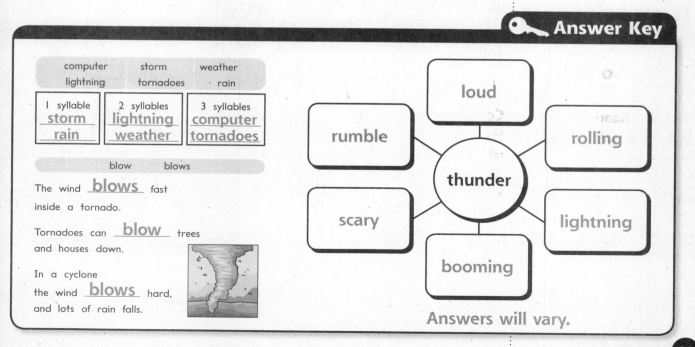

loud
rumble
rolling
thunder
scary
lightning
booming

Answers will vary.

Name_____

computer lightning	storm tornadoes	weather rain
1 syllable	2 syllables	3 syllables
_____ _____	_____ _____	_____ _____

blow   blows

The wind _____ fast

inside a tornado.

Tornadoes can _____ trees

and houses down.

In a cyclone

the wind _____ hard,

and lots of rain falls.

Stormy Weather PM Science Readers Teacher's Guide—Green Level

Name _____

Word Web

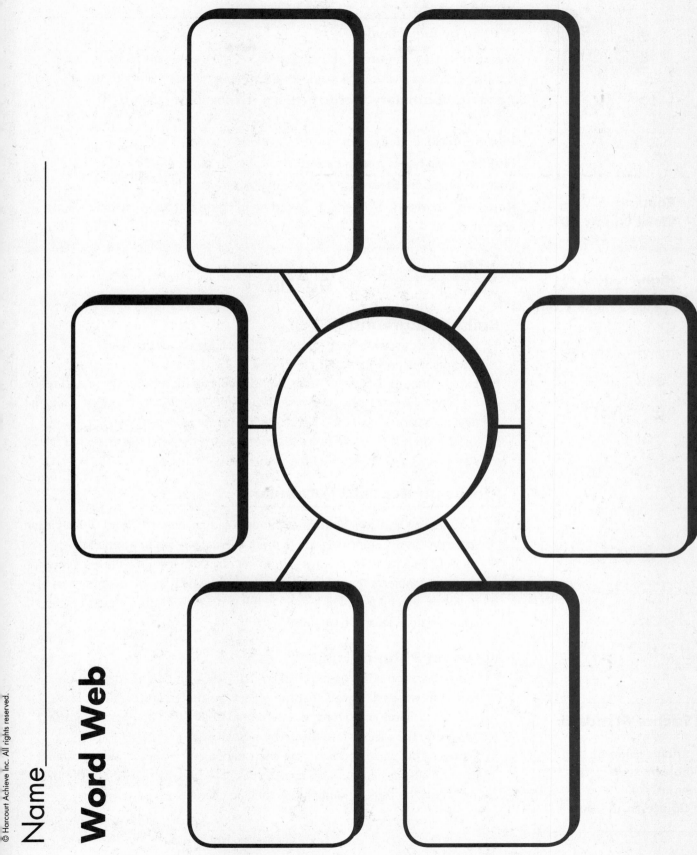

Reading Word Count: 207

Stars in the Sky

Written by Julie Haydon

Overview There are many stars in the sky. A star's color lets us know how hot it is. Our sun is a star. People use stars as guides and to draw pictures.

Reading Vocabulary Words hottest p. 4, coolest p. 5, ships p. 10, cloudy p. 11

Phonics Skill Endings: –est

Fluency Point Self-correcting errors

Comprehension Strategy Connecting text-to-text

Reading Strategy Skipping the word, reading on until end of sentence, and rereading

High-Frequency Words

give   small
how   than
need   their

1   Before Reading

Build Background

- Introduce the book by reading the title, talking about the cover photograph, and sharing the overview.
- Explain that readers sometimes skip difficult words in a sentence and read on. Say *If I keep reading, sometimes I can figure out a word by understanding the whole sentence. Then I can go back and reread the sentence again.*
- Ask children if they like to look at stars. Ask if they have ever seen a falling star. Have children describe the night sky.

Focus on Reading Vocabulary

- Write *hottest* and *coolest* on chart paper. Read each word aloud. Tell children these words are opposites. Have them use each word in a sentence.
- Model filling in a Word Sorter. Write *hottest* in the top box. Have children name two objects that are hot and write the words in the next level of boxes. Have children write words they associate with the objects on the appropriate side of the organizer.

Focus on Phonics Endings: –est

- Write *coolest* on chart paper. Explain that *–est* is an ending that can be added to words. It signals that the object has the greatest feature. Have each child name one word to describe an object that belongs to him or her. Write the adjective followed by *–est*.
- Write *big, hot, close,* and *bright* on chart paper. Ask *How can we write these words to describe our sun compared to other stars? Yes, we add –est.* Write the words on the paper, pointing out spelling changes.

Science Standard:

- **Knows some of the objects seen in the night sky**
- **Objects in the sky**

Focus on Fluency

- Read this sentence aloud: *Stars can be blue, white, yellow, orange, or red. The color of a star tells you how hot it is.* Say *I did not understand what this means. I will reread it again so I can understand it.*
- Have children select and read a page in the book. Ask them to stop and reread when they are confused by what they read.

Focus on Comprehension

- Explain that readers can connect what they read to other books they have read. Have children look at *We Need the Sun.* Ask *Do you remember what this book was about? Yes, it was about the sun keeping us warm and providing light.* Have children share what else they remember from *We Need the Sun.* Record their statements on chart paper.

2   Reading the Text

Book Talk

Cover   Read aloud the title with children. Point out the author's name. Talk about what the boy is looking at and the instrument he is using.

Pages 2–3   Ask *Do you notice that some stars are brighter than others? How far away do you think stars are? Yes, they are very far away from Earth.*

Pages 4–5   Say *I notice that the stars have different colors. What colors do you see? Yes, I see blue, red, orange, and white stars, too.*

Pages 6–7   Say *This picture shows the sun. What do you remember about the sun from* We Need the Sun? *Yes, it gives us warmth and light. Did you know the sun was a star?*

Pages 8–9   Ask *Which is bigger, the sun or Earth? Yes, the sun is bigger. Didn't we read about that in* We Need the Sun?

Pages 10–11   Say *In the drawing, the people in ships are looking up. What do you think they are looking at? Yes, probably the stars. Do you see stars in the photo on page 11? No, it is too cloudy to see them.*

Pages 12–13   Say *It looks like someone connected the stars like dots to draw a picture!* Ask *What pictures do these stars make?*

Pages 14–15   Say *Both of these photos show* **telescopes**. *Why do people use telescopes? Yes, it helps them to see objects that are far away. The big telescope is used by people who study the stars.*

ESL-ELL tip

Before reading the book, help children understand the difference between comparative and superlative. Show children three colors of stars: a blue star, a yellow star, and a red star. Say *The blue star is the hottest star. The red star is the coolest star.* Explain that –est is used to compare three or more objects.

Reading Strategy

Remind children of the skills and strategies when assistance is needed. Say *Sometimes you have to skip over a word you don't know and keep reading. You might find clues in the rest of the sentence to help you figure out the meaning of an unfamiliar word.*

Individual Reading

Have each child read the whole book at his or her own pace while remaining in the group. Observe children as they read. Make note, mentally or in writing, how each child is or is not using the skills and strategies being focused on in this lesson:

1. Are children able to identify and read the reading vocabulary words without assistance?
2. Are children able to add –*est* endings to adjectives?
3. Are children self-correcting as they read to improve their comprehension and fluency?
4. Are children making text-to-text connections while reading?
5. Are children skipping difficult words and reading on and rereading to improve comprehension?

3 Text Reading Review

Reading Vocabulary Review

- Have children write *ships* on a piece of paper. Read aloud. On the back of their paper, have children draw different kinds of ships. Children can take turns displaying their ships to the group.
- Have children highlight, or add, the reading vocabulary words in their copies of *My PM Word Book*. Encourage children to use these words in their writing.

Phonics Review

Write *slowest* on chart paper. Have children find words in the book that end in –*est* (*hottest* p. 4, *coolest* p. 5, *closest* p. 8). Add to the chart paper. Have children brainstorm a list of other words that end in –*est*. Write their responses on the chart paper.

Fluency Review

Have children reread the book in pairs. Partners can alternate reading pages. Remind children to reread words, sentences, or pages that they do not understand.

Comprehension Review

Have children look through *We Need the Sun* and *Stars in the Sky*. Have partners share what they learned from both books. Remind children that making connections between different texts helps with their reading.

Connection for Writing

Tell children to date the page of a blank journal. Say *Today you are going to write a journal page about looking at the stars. Write about a place where the stars are bright. Describe the place, what you saw, and how you felt.*

Connect to Math

PM Math Readers
Snail Trail to 100
(Set 16–17)
With children, plot points of "star pictures" to make their own pictures. Number each star using a 100s chart.

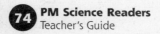

4 Assessment and Practice

Reading Vocabulary Application

Provide children with a Word Sorter with the word *coolest* in the top box. Work with children to name two things that are cool to the touch in the next level of boxes. Have children describe each object on the appropriate side of the organizer.

Phonics Evaluation

Write *–est* on chart paper. Individually, have each child create a list of four words that end in *–est* on a sheet of paper.

Fluency Assessment

Individually, have each child read the story to you. Listen to make sure children are self-correcting errors in reading to aid in fluency.

Comprehension Check

Individually, have each child share one fact that he or she learned from *We Need the Sun* that was also discussed in *Stars in the Sky*.

Independent Practice

- Have children practice the high-frequency words found within this title using the matching PM High-Frequency Word Cards.
- Provide children with a copy of the activity sheet. Give directions on how to complete the activity sheet. Have children complete the sheet independently.

Differentiated Instruction

- **Kinesthetic** learners can "feel" the story by making a shoe-box planetarium.
- **Auditory** learners can "hear" the story by listening to someone else reading the book to them.
- **Visual** learners can "see" the story by drawing their own star pictures.

Answer Key

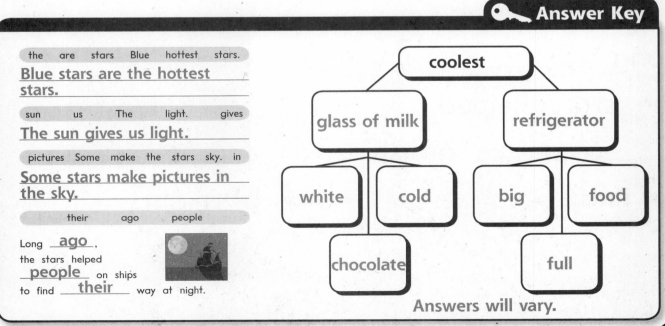

the are stars Blue hottest stars.

Blue stars are the hottest stars.

sun us The light. gives

The sun gives us light.

pictures Some make the stars sky. in

Some stars make pictures in the sky.

their ago people

Long __ago__,
the stars helped
__people__ on ships
to find __their__ way at night.

coolest

glass of milk — refrigerator

white — cold — big — food

chocolate — full

Answers will vary.

Name_____

the   are   stars   Blue   hottest   stars.

_____

_____

sun   us   The   light.   gives

_____

_____

pictures   Some   make   the   stars   sky.   in

_____

_____

their   ago   people

Long _____,
the stars helped
_____ on ships
to find _____ way at night.

Stars in the Sky PM Science Readers Teacher's Guide—Green Level

Name

Word Sorter

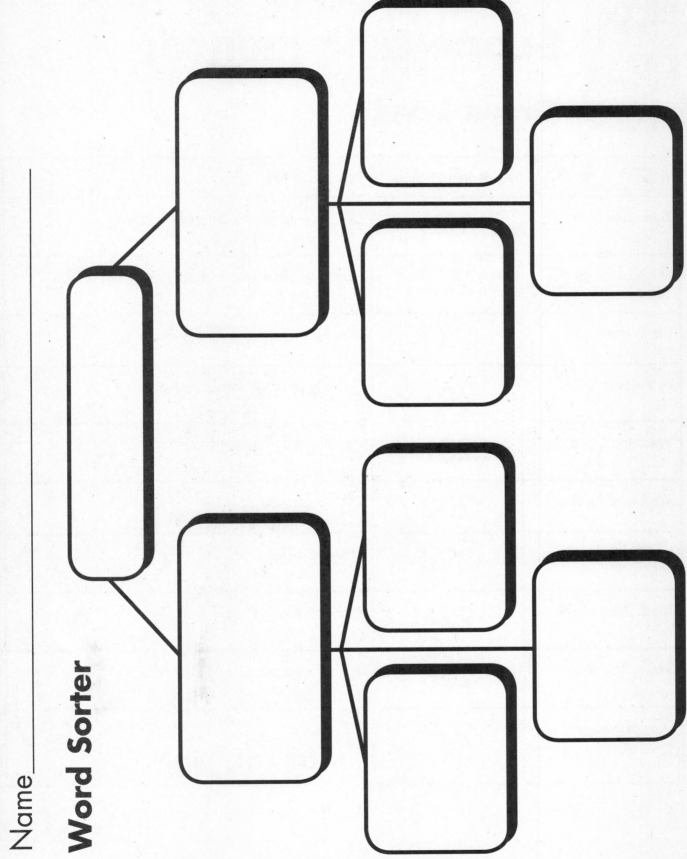

Scope & Sequence:

Green Level

Title	Running Words	Phonics Skill	
Rocks and Earth	196	Use knowledge of spelling patterns: CVCe	
My Book of the Seasons	271	Changing phonemes to make new words	
Life in Hot Places	247	Identifying and segmenting syllables	
By the Sea	251	Demonstrate understanding of plurals	
Watching Clouds	201	Reading high-frequency words	
We Need the Sun	202	Compound words	
Looking at the Moon	228	Consonant blend: *pl*	
The Coldest Places	224	Root words	
Stormy Weather	208	Using knowledge of syllables to decode multiple-syllable words	
Stars in the Sky	207	Endings: *est*	

Fluency Point	Comprehension Strategy	Reading Strategy
Adjusting pace	Classifying and categorizing information	Looking at the pictures
Using softness or loudness to express emotion	Connecting ideas: text-to-self	Thinking about what comes next and if it makes sense
Pausing at commas	Comparing and contrasting	Using punctuation as you read
Reading every word without skipping or substituting words	Visualizing information from text, illustrations, diagrams, etc.	Pointing to each word as you read
Varying the use of intonation when reading phrases	Making generalizations	Looking at the end of the word
Reading smoothly	Connecting ideas: text-to-self	Checking for a pattern
Taking a breath at appropriate times	Drawing conclusions	Looking at the picture and the word's first letter
Using strategies to pronounce unknown words	Building background knowledge	Getting your mouth ready for the first letter's sound
Voice falling at the end of declarative sentence	Recognizing cause and effect	Sounding it out
Self-correcting errors	Connecting ideas: text-to-text	Skipping the word, reading on until the end of a sentence, and rereading